IN THE GARDEN

GARDEN

of His Grace

By Teresa E. Lavergne

ISBN: 0996623736
ISBN-13: 9780996623735

These devotions come from notes written in my journals as I read God's Word in the morning. I pray they will refresh your spirit, give you new perspectives on things Jesus said and did, and help you see Jesus and His great heart of love, mercy, and compassion for you in a brand new way.

Originally I shared these as posts on the internet, but after receiving requests to have them in a book, I set out to accomplish that with the Lord's help.

Then I found that there were too many to make one book, so there will be several volumes to complete the project.

Thank you Debbie and Ronald Boudreaux
for sharing your lovely garden with me
for the cover photo of this book.

THE INVITATION

Come into His garden----He is waiting there for you.

He invites you to walk with Him there.

There is Joy in His presence....a river of delights runs through this garden.

He will replace your filthy rags with His clothes of righteousness.....and you will be beautiful in His sight.

He will fill you with His glory----His Holy Spirit, and your face will shine with His love.

He calls you out of the land of dark shadows into His light, where His truth dwells and heals your mind.

Your soul is satisfied in belonging to Him, for His goodness exceeds imagination.

All the wounds of your past are healed by His touch.

He will protect you forever, and will never desert you.

Your guilt and shame are gone.

You mean everything to Him; He left His home to seek you out and rescue you, when you were trapped in the dungeon of sin.

He paid the price to set you free.

Come into His garden----He wants to be with you.

"I have loved you with an everlasting love;
Therefore I have drawn you with lovingkindness.....

And their life will be like a watered garden,
And they will never languish again.

And My people will be satisfied with My goodness," declares
the LORD.

from Jeremiah 31: portions of verses 3, 12, and 14 NASB

HIS NAME

"You shall call His name Jesus." Matthew 1:21 NASB

His name was the clue---the evidence that confirmed to Mary that Joseph had indeed been informed by a heavenly messenger about the child conceived within her.

Mary was in a very uncomfortable situation----she was pregnant and unmarried without any proof that she had not been promiscuous. Her fiancée did not believe her story. We don't know if anyone else did, either. Her declaration must have sounded preposterous to most.

Mary desperately needed someone to believe in her and care for her.

The name of Jesus that was given to her by the angel was now also given to Joseph. He was in on the secret now---- and he believed.

The shame and isolation she must have felt, was eased by the partnership with Joseph. He bore her shame, too, when he took her to be his wife.

In doing so, he received great honor from God----he became the earthly parent to God's Son. When Joseph said yes to the disgrace this situation would bring him, he in turn received the honor of having Jesus live in his home.

"For those who exalt themselves will be humbled, and those who humble themselves will be exalted." Matthew 23:12

When we belong to the Lord, we may sometimes have to endure shame and disgrace for His sake, but he is not ashamed to call us His family. Hebrews 2:11

It is only if we become ashamed of Him that He would deny us, or disclaim us. Luke 9:26

Choose wisely; never forfeit your heavenly destiny for earthly prominence or acclaim. Romans 1:16

If we bear His name, and yet do things that are unlike His character----that do not have His trademark----we dishonor His glorious name. May we live in a manner worthy of His name.

"Lord, our Lord, how majestic is your name in all the earth!" Psalm 8:9

"Salvation is found in no one else, for there is no other name under heaven given to mankind by which we must be saved." Acts 4:12

"Therefore God exalted him to the highest place and gave him the name that is above every name," Philippians 2:9

"In his name the nations will put their hope." Matthew 12:21

"You have exalted above all else Your name and Your word" from Psalm 138:2 AMPC

OPEN OUR EYES

Jesus took three of his disciples and went up on the mountain. It was there that those three got a glimpse of Jesus in His heavenly glory.

They had fallen asleep, and as they were waking up, they saw Jesus shining with a brilliant light---shining with the glory He had with the Father before time began!

There were two men talking with Him; somehow the disciples knew it was Moses and Elijah. In his confusion, Peter blurted out something he thought was reverent---but he made no distinction between Jesus and the two prophets. So God did. When the disciples heard God's voice coming out of heaven, they fell down as if paralyzed with fear.

Then Jesus touched them, and said "Don't be afraid." I am so comforted in seeing how He touched people--- compassion is in His touch.

"When they opened their eyes, they saw only Jesus." Matthew 17: 8 CEV

And they were changed.

"The Word became flesh and made his dwelling among us. We have seen his glory, the glory of the one and only Son, who came from the Father, full of grace and truth." John 1:14

The more we see Jesus as He truly is, the more we are changed.

"But we all, with unveiled face, beholding as in a mirror the glory of the Lord, are being transformed into the same image from glory to glory, just as by the Spirit of the Lord."
2 Corinthians 3:18 NKJV

Jesus said, "The one who looks at me is seeing the one who sent me." John 12:45

"So we have stopped evaluating others from a human point of view. At one time we thought of Christ merely from a human point of view. How differently we know him now!"
2 Corinthians 5:16 NLT

When we see Jesus, we see others from His perspective.

He is looking forward to the time when we all will see His glory.

"Father, I want those you have given me to be with me where I am, and to see my glory, the glory you have given me because you loved me before the creation of the world."
John 17:24

We need to be looking at Jesus, the author and finisher of our faith.

"Look, he is coming with the clouds...." Revelation 1:7

Until then,

"Open my eyes, so that I may see the wonderful truths in your law." Psalm 119:18 GNT

A ROSE AT NIGHT

Darkness and evil hung over the Garden of Gethsemane that night, but there was also a Presence there more beautiful than any other, and a fragrance more poignant than words. Satan and all his demon hordes laughed and jeered at the Man kneeling in prayer in the moonlight. They knew what was coming.

Thousands of years before, a terrible decision was made in a garden that brought doom upon this earth. This planet was meant to be a place of celestial delight, but the Deceitful one was so enraged by his jealousy that he made plans to destroy the recipients of this attention. He never dreamed that what he mocked would be his undoing.

Christ's unending, unconditional love is the signature characteristic of the Kingdom of God. It is who He is, and the Kingdom of God operates through this Love. Satan cannot comprehend it, and neither can the kingdoms of this world.

At the Cross, God's mercy triumphed through this Love, and Satan lost in his game of deceit and treachery. Jesus' love was the trump card He played that fateful day, and His resurrection the surprise ending to that game of fate.

Jesus Christ foiled Satan's plan to enslave us forever to sin, and to have us sentenced to the flames of hell. Our doom is no longer sealed because Christ's tomb could not be kept sealed!

All of us who have put our faith in His unchanging Love are now sealed by the Holy Spirit for redemption. We are citizens of Heaven.

"Follow God's example, therefore, as dearly loved children and walk in the way of love, just as Christ loved us and gave himself up for us as a fragrant offering and sacrifice to God." Ephesians 5:1-2

"And you also were included in Christ when you heard the message of truth, the gospel of your salvation. When you believed, you were marked in him with a seal, the promised Holy Spirit, who is a deposit guaranteeing our inheritance until the redemption of those who are God's possession—to the praise of his glory." Ephesians 1:13-14

"Praise be to the God and Father of our Lord Jesus Christ! In his great mercy he has given us new birth into a living hope through the resurrection of Jesus Christ from the dead, and into an inheritance that can never perish, spoil or fade. This inheritance is kept in heaven for you, who through faith are shielded by God's power until the coming of the salvation that is ready to be revealed in the last time." I Peter 1:3-5

"Now it is God who makes both us and you stand firm in Christ. He anointed us, set his seal of ownership on us, and put his Spirit in our hearts as a deposit, guaranteeing what is to come." 2 Corinthians 1:21-22

THE HEART BEHIND THE WALL

The story of the Battle of Jericho, and how the wall fell down, never seems to lose its thrill for children. We told and reenacted that Bible story many times and in many ways over the years. But recently I found myself thinking about Rahab.

She had heard of the power of the God of the Israelites and of what He had done to rescue His people from the Egyptians.

Was it only her fear that prompted her to hide the two Israelite spies who came into Jericho? Was it only survival instinct that made her barter for her life---or was it something more?

We don't know the names of the two spies Joshua sent into Jericho, but we do know the name of the Israelite man who married Rahab. His name was Salmon. Some people have wondered if Salmon was one of those spies.

I have wondered under what circumstances Rahab married this Israelite man---was she a prisoner of war, or one of the spoils of war? If so, she and her family were the only ones--- all other inhabitants of their city were destroyed.

Yet she married an Israelite—one of the people group who were responsible for destroying her city---including her neighbors and acquaintances.

Is it possible that Rahab was already looking for a way to get out of Jericho---a way to be rescued from a life of prostitution? She knew the sordid side of sex---the marketed

9

kind. Perhaps Rahab was longing for a husband and children---and for the love of a man who truly cared for her and who wasn't using her.

Could it be that there was already a longing in her heart to belong to such a God as this, who cared about His people and delivered them from slavery?

And God, who sees all hearts, looked into this heart behind the wall and knew what she desired---and granted it because of her faith.

It would be no accident then that the spies ended up at <u>her</u> house. She told the spies, "for the Lord your God is God in heaven above and on the earth below."

Rahab's house was built into the city wall. When the wall collapsed, Joshua told his men to go into Rahab's house and bring her and her family out to safety. That means that when the wall collapsed, one small part didn't---the part that contained Rahab's house.

And this house had to be rather high on the wall since Rahab helped the spies escape down a rope hung from a window.

One specific tall narrow section of the massive wall must have been left standing after the entire wall around the city collapsed. Only God could have done that feat. What greater evidence of God's favor could there be?

This Israelite Salmon, who married the prostitute Rahab, had a son by her. His name was Boaz. And if you have read the story of Ruth, you know what a kind and thoughtful man Boaz was. Yet he was an older man when he met Ruth; why had he never married?

Perhaps there was a social stigma and prejudice involved. His mother had been a prostitute and she was not Hebrew.

Maybe this is part of the reason he had compassion for Ruth; she too was a foreigner from a country of low reputation.

She was from the land of Moab, and some thought there was a curse on Moab and its inhabitants. Boaz must have learned about mercy and humility from his parents.

This brings me to a wonderful realization. The people that society rejects are often the people who God accepts and writes into His story.

There they are in Matthew's genealogy of the lineage of Christ: Salmon, Rahab, Boaz and Ruth. (Matthew 1:5)

And another thing: when God says He will tear down a wall, nothing can stand in His way. He knows what is in the heart behind the wall, and He is the Savior.

"For Christ himself has brought peace to us. He united Jews and Gentiles into one people when, in his own body on the cross, he broke down the wall of hostility that separated us.

He did this by ending the system of law with its commandments and regulations.

He made peace between Jews and Gentiles by creating in himself one new people from the two groups."

Ephesians 2:14-15 NLT

SEE THE WORLD

How many times have you heard someone say "I want to see the world"? People have traveled around the globe by boat, plane, or more primitive means in order to see the world.

Jesus wants us to see the world------through His eyes.

How does He see it? In His eyes, everyone is a prisoner of sin.

"But the Scriptures declare that we are all prisoners of sin, so we receive God's promise of freedom only by believing in Jesus Christ." Galatians 3:22 NLT

In His eyes, the whole world is under the control of the evil one.

"We know that we are children of God, and that the whole world is under the control of the evil one. We know also that the Son of God has come and has given us understanding, so that we may know him who is true. And we are in him who is true by being in his Son Jesus Christ. He is the true God and eternal life." 1 John 5:19-20

Christianity is not a religion or belief system---it is that, only to those who have made it so. To be a Christian means that you have had an encounter with Christ---in person.

It does not mean you assented to a set of beliefs. That will make you religious, but not a Christian.

What sets Christianity apart is that it is not based on a dead man's sayings; it is based on a Living Person and Words that are alive, with supernatural power from Christ.

Seeing the world from Jesus' viewpoint will make you into a "radical" thinker. An encounter with Christ will change you and the way you look at the world.

"So from now on we regard no one from a worldly point of view. Though we once regarded Christ in this way, we do so no longer.

Therefore, if anyone is in Christ, the new creation has come: The old has gone, the new is here!

All this is from God, who reconciled us to himself through Christ and gave us the ministry of reconciliation: that God was reconciling the world to himself in Christ, not counting people's sins against them. And he has committed to us the message of reconciliation.

We are therefore Christ's ambassadors, as though God were making his appeal through us. We implore you on Christ's behalf: Be reconciled to God.

God made him who had no sin to be sin for us, so that in him we might become the righteousness of God."
2 Corinthians 5:16-21

This is the viewpoint of Jesus.

When we encounter Him, and begin a relationship with Him, we are made into a different sort of human: our viewpoint of life, and the purpose of existence, is forever changed.

COME HOME

We can become so enshrouded, so enveloped, so encapsulated by the negative words spoken of us, that the Lord's words of good intentions towards us are hindered from penetrating this cocoon around our minds.

Rejection by people makes it harder to believe that the Lord actually wants to lavish His favor on us.

Deep within, we instinctively feel that if we do not measure up, or if we have not achieved this "level of acceptance", we will not have His favor.

When we evaluate ourselves by estimations of other people, we begin to think that the Lord only tolerates us as well.

We forget the passion that motivated His sacrifice of Himself for us, and downgrade His motives to "religious duty".

The story of the Prodigal Son gives us a different picture.

When the Prodigal Son returned, though he WAS guilty of squandering his father's grace, the father lavished gifts of approval on him!

Jesus told this story so that we would not doubt the nature of our God. Like every good father, He disciplines His children, but this does not diminish His desire for good things for us. He is not like earthly fathers who discount, dislike, and discard their very own children. He believes in us-----that with His help, we are capable of greatness.

I think the older brother in the story represents people in the Kingdom of God who become self-righteous and resentful of the gifts the Lord lavishes on others. They feel His favor has to be deserved by correct behavior or some kind of merit. In their eyes, the prodigal son did not meet these requirements; he had done nothing worthy of the father's attention.

The older brother probably wanted the prodigal son to go away again, or be excluded, or be demoted in status. He certainly did not want him to have the father's blessings! But the story shows us the father's love for his children.

The father wanted the older brother to rejoice that the family was reunited and together again. This shows what is important to the Father. The older brother was thinking only about himself, instead of rejoicing to see his father so happy. The father's concerns were not his; the father's delight should have made him glad.

The older brother must have thought the prodigal son had forfeited all his relationships forever, but the father treated the younger son with dignity and compassion---not with scorn and revulsion, as the older brother did.

The father never condoned the sinful desires which caused the separation, but love was freely given when the son came home. Yet the older brother resented the father for this.

There is a huge contrast between the nature of the father in the story, and the nature of the older brother. The older brother represents religion—based on earning favor--- and the father represents the gift of God's grace.

We are God's children, and He desires the best for us----not what the worldly culture says is best----HIS best. Don't stay at a distance from Him, doubting His love and fearful of rejection. Come close to Him----He will run to meet you with open arms!

Jesus came to reveal the Father to us---to show us what the Father is like. Let your thinking and your feelings be shaped by the words of Jesus---His righteousness is never wrong.

"Philip said, "'Lord, show us the Father and that will be enough for us.'" Jesus answered: "Don't you know me, Philip, even after I have been among you such a long time? Anyone who has seen me has seen the Father. How can you say, 'Show us the Father'?"   John 14:8-9

"In the past God spoke to our ancestors through the prophets at many times and in various ways, but in these last days he has spoken to us by his Son, whom he appointed heir of all things, and through whom also he made the universe. The Son is the radiance of God's glory and the exact representation of his being, sustaining all things by his powerful word. After he had provided purification for sins, he sat down at the right hand of the Majesty in heaven." Hebrews 1:1-3

HIS PATH

You are our shepherd, Lord. You give us what we need.

We cannot survive without You.

We cannot go off on our own without becoming lost, because You ARE the Way, the Truth, and the Life. The only reliable path is Yours.

All other paths lead to dead ends---they end in death and destruction.

"The path of the righteous is like the morning sun, shining ever brighter till the full light of day." Proverbs 4:18

"He guides me in the paths of righteousness for His name's sake." Psalm 23:3 NASB

This must be a path of Mercy, or goodness and mercy would not be able to follow us there

"Surely goodness and mercy shall follow me all the days of my life...." Ps. 23:6 NKJV

When we get off the goodness-and-mercy path, our service to God becomes more like a means of achieving status and rank; it becomes hollow, static, and artificial. We're just doing the expected thing to fit in to the group.

"Seek first his kingdom and his righteousness" Matthew 6:33

This is our compass--it keeps our heart and motivations in line with His will.

With His Word directing our hearts, we will stay on His path.

One day He will conquer the whole world and rule from sea to sea. We will see His glory and all His majesty!

But the most magnificent thing to me is that He has conquered my unruly heart and made it His possession.

And when I yielded to His love, I found not only a Savior and Lord, but a Friend who cares about me intimately.

I found the Shepherd of my heart.

Our Shepherd provides a refuge for us; a shady place to rest from the heat of the day's battles. When you are battle weary, seek out this refuge.

It is like an oasis in the desert where you can find the living water that refreshes and strengthens you on your journey through life.

Go often to this special place; Jesus will meet you there.

He satisfies our desires with good things. (from Psalm 103:5)

ONLY JESUS

Only Jesus.......can satisfy your deepest longings for
      significance.

Only Jesus...... can make the puzzle pieces of your Life fit
      together.

Only Jesus...... can bring you safely through the storms that
      lie ahead.

Only Jesus...... can give you Wisdom that you need in all
      your relationships.

Only Jesus...... can give you grace to overcome selfishness
      and pride.

Only Jesus...... can give you a love so strong that you can
      forgive those who hate you and hurt you.

Only Jesus...... can prepare you for Eternity.

He is our Hope.

"In His name the nations will put their hope." Matthew 12:21

A MOTHER'S PRAYER

May you always value:

True friendship over great popularity,

Character more than wealth,

Humility more than renown,

Real love more than stubborn pride,

Faithfulness more than personal success,

Long-lasting wisdom more than temporary pleasures,

Restraint more than rashness,

Peace more than harshness,

Forgiveness more than power to hurt,

and God's principles more than the opinions of the world.

May you value diligence over indulgence,

Kindness over strife, true beauty over lust,

Patience over anger, intimacy over possessions,

Faith over negative thinking, meekness over self-will,

Passion over fear, and genuine purity over image.

In short, may you value Jesus and all he is, over all the attractions in this world.

THINGS I LEARNED FROM A CHILD

Jesus told us to become like little children.

What? Did He really mean that?

Did He mean:

Fight over toys and refuse to share?

Dominate people----"I was here first"?

Bite to express anger?

Throw a tantrum when you can't have your way?

Resist authority when you can't have what you want because it is bad for your body?

Become extremely impatient when waiting for anything---especially food?

And struggle when you're being cleaned and changed?

No.

I believe He means this:

Never lose the wonder of your existence; you are God's most marvelous creation.

Sing to the Lord just because you can; you don't need a reason other than God is good.

Rejoice in simple things, like a floating feather, or a sunbeam on the floor. God made this world for you.

Be content if you are dry, fed, and loved. Trust in God's care of you; He's your Daddy.

Don't be reserved and ashamed to show emotion; laugh with others, and cry with others.

Keep learning and discovering all the things that you can do. God has plans for you.

Clap for yourself and cheer yourself on. God is cheering for you all the way.

Enjoy people even on their ugliest days, just because they love you.

Start over every day; forgive what happened yesterday because it's already forgotten. Only today is important.

THE HEART OF DAVID

The Lord said "I have found David son of Jesse, a man after my own heart," Acts 13:22

What was it about David that made the Lord say this?

I think I'm beginning to understand.

What kind of man would go after a bear and a lion, to save a sheep? What kind of man would risk his life over that? One lamb, is after all, not that important or valuable---and easily replaced. Some would say David's actions were foolish.

But these sheep were under David's care. He could not ignore that lamb's cry for help when it looked to him. David had a heart of compassion that caused him to fight off any enemy of his flock. He was a good shepherd.

When David saw that giant of a man threatening God's people, he could not ignore it. No one was protecting God's flock----so David did.

He had faith in God's faithfulness---he believed that the Lord would be with him, even though he was an insignificant person.

Some looked at that faith, and called it arrogance, conceit, and delusion.

But the Lord saw a man that exhibited His character. That was the kind of man that God wanted---the kind of man who would take care of His people.

King Saul was more concerned about protecting his own reputation, instead of God's. It became evident that he cared more about what people thought about him, than what God thought about him.

Jesus called Himself the Good Shepherd, who lays down His life for the sheep. When the enemy threatens, you can be sure that Jesus hears your cry and will come to your rescue.

It may not always be in the way that you thought He would---His ways are higher than ours. He will never leave you or forsake you---He will be our Shepherd, our guide forever.

"For this God is our God for ever and ever; he will be our guide even to the end." Psalm 48:14

"The Lord is my Shepherd, I lack nothing." Psalm 23:1

He is everything we need.

DELIGHT

"You prepare a table before me in the presence of my enemies. You anoint my head with oil; my cup overflows." Psalm 23:5

"I have loved you with an everlasting love; I have drawn you with unfailing kindness" Jeremiah 31:3

There will always be oppressors---these are the people who do not want you to think of yourself as valuable in God's eyes, because they do not.

The scorn can either bring you to despair---or it can cause you to find a place of refuge in Jesus; a place of intimacy and security in His love.

Those who have lived with rejection for long periods of time, may find it hard to believe that Jesus actually likes them.

Mentally, the fact of His sacrificial death on their behalf is accepted; but esteem has been so long denied them that they cannot seem to fully grasp the reality of His favor.

They continue to feel they are too stupid, too ugly, too lacking in every area.

The oppressors in their lives agree with this assessment, and try to instill in them the notion that it would be arrogance to think God prizes them, or desires them.

And yet, He does. From the moment you were born, He did. He delights in you more than a loving mother or father ever could.

His passion is to win you to Himself, so that He can spend an eternity with you.

He had these words recorded about Himself in His book so that you would know this is true:

"the Lord delights in those who fear him, who put their hope in his unfailing love." Psalm 147:11.

"The Lord your God is with you, the Mighty Warrior who saves. He will take great delight in you; in his love he will no longer rebuke you, but will rejoice over you with singing." Zephaniah 3:17.

We can dare to say that He delights in us!

If you realize that you have been playing the part of an oppressor, that your reactions to others are typically harsh and critical, ask the Lord to help you see others through the eyes of His favor. The verb favor means to "value, prize, and esteem."

This crazy world is so full of its own opinions, it is revolting. I choose the Lord's opinion, and His mindset!

In His eyes, every person is extremely valuable. No matter what others think of you, the Lord delights in you!

DEEP AS THE OCEAN

"There is the sea, vast and spacious, teeming with creatures beyond number—living things both large and small." Psalm 104:25

God's love for us is like the ocean----far more powerful than we can imagine----so vast we have never fully explored it, and so deep that there are things in it we have never seen.

The ocean is full of life---so varied and vast in number that we could never stop growing in our knowledge of it. And so it is with God's love---there is no end to His capacity to love. We need His love; we were born to need it.

"And I pray that you, being rooted and established in love, may have power, together with all the Lord's holy people, to grasp how wide and long and high and deep is the love of Christ, and to know this love that surpasses knowledge— that you may be filled to the measure of all the fullness of God." Ephesians 3:17-19

A shallow, superficial existence based only on fulfilling human desires can never satisfy us like an intimate spirit-to-spirit relationship with the Lord. And out of that intimacy there will spring forth new spiritual life that brings beauty into the world---it flows out to others with waves of God's glory. It is moving; it is never stagnant.

"Deep calls to deep in the roar of your waterfalls; all your waves and breakers have swept over me." Psalm 42:7

His love is calling you....... Go deeper still.

A VALENTINE BETTER THAN CHOCOLATE!

Did you ever eat dark chocolate to stay awake?

It seems to work for me. (And dark chocolate is one of my favorite foods)

But I have wondered how we stay awake spiritually---and I have come to the conclusion that it is God's love that keeps the Church spiritually "awake".

The "Church" refers to every group of believers who worship together and work together to make Christ known.

God's love is the energy source---the fuel---for the Church.

It is like the oil in our lamps; unless we replenish it, our light for Christ grows dim. Luke 12:35

We can't manufacture it; we receive it through continual sincere prayer and heartfelt worship.

Jesus is our example in this. During his earthly ministry, Jesus demonstrated His dependence on the Heavenly Father for His confidence and strength.

Love flowed out from Jesus to other people, because of His trust in His Heavenly Father's love of Him. He demonstrated His relationship of love with the Heavenly Father.

Confidence in the way God loves us grows from our relationship with Him. We maintain this by seeking Him, and then His light grows brighter and stronger in us.

God's love can't flow out from us, if we are not confident in the sure reality that He loves us personally and unconditionally and indefinitely.

Without God's love as the energy source, the people of God become sluggish.

"Dear friends, since God so loved us, we also ought to love one another. No one has ever seen God; but if we love one another, God lives in us and his love is made complete in us." 1 John 4:11-12

"….God's love has been poured out into our hearts through the Holy Spirit, who has been given to us." Romans 5:5

All of God's Word is like one big Valentine.

He loves us; now we can love each other.

Then His light will shine.

THE KEY

Jesus is the only One who has the key to our hearts.

He is the only One who can unlock it and free us from the prison of Self.

When some are wounded by the words of others, often their hearts are imprisoned in the dungeon of discouragement.

Others are so afraid of being vulnerable, that they harden their hearts and become imprisoned behind its walls.

But it is in our weakness that we become strong, for it is our weakness that causes us to depend upon the Lord's strength.

He always knows exactly what we are thinking in our hearts. (Luke 5:22 is an example)

He knows what we think about ourselves.

He knows what we are thinking about this person or that person.

We cannot hide anything in our hearts from Him.

He knows us----not just our names or that we exist;

He knows who we are.....who we truly are.

He knows every detail about our lives. Psalm 139:1-16

He also knows who we are supposed to become.

He is the Key to finding this.

NON-SENSE

I don't know why we put more credence in what people say about ourselves, than in what God says. It makes much more sense to believe the opinion of the one who created us---the one who designed us!

People say things like "You're not enough; you don't measure up." God says, "Trust me and see what you can do!"

"Trust in the Lord with all your heart; do not depend on your own understanding." Proverbs 3:5-6 NLT He is able to do far more than we can imagine or think. His possibilities are limitless, because He has no limits! Matthew 19:26

"Now to him who is able to do immeasurably more than all we ask or imagine, according to his power that is at work within us, to him be glory in the church and in Christ Jesus throughout all generations, for ever and ever! Amen." Ephesians 3:20-21

David was a shepherd boy who trusted in God's opinion more than in the opinions of people. He had seen what faith could do---he had already faced a lion and a bear.

When he saw Goliath, he knew God's power could bring down that giant. People told David that he couldn't do it; that it was very foolish for him to think of it. They looked at the giant, and then looked at him, and in their eyes, David was not enough. He didn't measure up.

David's own family did not value his faith or his judgment. He was young and small, and they thought very little of him.

They were critical of him, because they did not trust his motives.

Even leaders did not believe in him at first, but he did not let this daunt him. Those who were trying to discourage him did not realize they were disparaging the providence of God.

We always speak of David's courage in facing the giant---- but it also took great courage to go against the opinions of so many people.

He was among seasoned warriors and experienced fighters, as well as the king of Israel and his military advisors.

His own brothers, who were in the army, were angry with him, viewing him as rash and impudent. They were embarrassed and ashamed of their brother.

But David knew what God had spoken to him. Against all this opposition from his own side, he determinedly went in search of five small rocks.

He faced the mockery of the giant on one side, and the scornful disbelief on the other. I am so thankful that David chose to believe what God said. When others said, "You can't", God said, "You can."

If David had believed what people said instead of what God said, the Israelites would have been enslaved by Philistines---a God-hating, idolatrous, child-sacrificing people.

Lord, give us some Davids to fight the "giants" in our land.

It just might be you.

NO CIRCLES

"I instruct you in the way of wisdom and lead you along straight paths." Proverbs 4:11

Jesus said we are like sheep. We need a shepherd. Sheep can get off the right path and get lost; they sometimes lay down and can't get up; they are easy victims for predators; they consume things that make them internally ill; or they can wander away and fall off of cliffs.

Jesus said His sheep would know His voice and follow Him. John 10:1-5 & 14-16 We need to make it a practice daily to listen for His voice, so we can recognize it better. He speaks through His Word; this is who He is.

"Blessed are those who listen to me, watching daily at my doors, waiting at my doorway." Proverbs 8:34

There are general instructions for all of us sheep, but He also has specific instructions for us. We need to listen carefully and pay attention, and focus on what He tells us. John 21:17-22

Human nature causes people to be motivated by the desire to "fit in". If human desires overrule what the Holy Spirit desires, there is a subtle shift from following Jesus to a priority of "fitting in". People begin to follow each other, instead of our chief Shepherd, Jesus. They conform to the expectations and perceptions of the group.

This is why prayer is so vital and necessary---to grow the culture of the Kingdom of God. Beware of the yeast of the Pharisees---it will grow a religious culture, not one of Heaven. Matthew 16:12 John 5:44

Beware of those who come dressed like a sheep---but when they speak, it is the voice of a wolf. They sound more like Wall Street than the Heavenly Way.   Matthew 7:15

"But you, dear friends, by building yourselves up in your most holy faith and praying in the Holy Spirit, keep yourselves in God's love as you wait for the mercy of our Lord Jesus Christ to bring you to eternal life." Jude 20-21.

OUR FATHER

Lord, I am so thankful that You are not like the temperamental so-called "gods" of the ancient world. You are a God who welcomes us and washes the feet of those You love.

We need to remember that You are a God who cares when even a tiny sparrow falls and dies. We are worth far more than a sparrow to You.

He is not a hard-hearted, heavy-handed Sovereign we must submit to out of cringing fear. He is a Person who longs for intimacy with His creation. He wants to be family to us---not just a holy Sovereign, but a loving Father.

"Take delight in the Lord"----look at Jesus----what He says and does, and you will see the Father. It is a delight to look at Jesus and see what the Father is truly like.

We can't be in love with "churchianity" or a religious social club. We can only have a love relationship with a Person. Think of this---the most famous Person in the world wants you to know Him intimately!

What He will impart to you through knowing Him is what people through the ages always search for: significance for their existence, and life beyond the grave.

Lord, help us to value intimacy with You more than the esteem from other people, and help us to respect each other's relationship with Christ. This is a holy thing we should never trample on, or treat shamefully.

Seeking the Lord is an active pursuit; it is a determined effort we must exercise continually because of the decadence and deception all around us. We live in an atmosphere of lies, in this fallen world.

The most terrifying words of all are these: "I don't know you." Seek to know Him, so that He will never have a reason to say this to you!

The more that we know Him, the more we will trust Him. If we trust in His loving character, we know that we can talk to Him about every concern we have, and He will not despise us.

He already knows what is in our hearts; we can't pretend with Him. He knows our every thought and every word we will say before we say it! Psalm 139:2-4

The more we know Him, we will want people to know His true character, just as Jesus wanted people to see the Father in Him and what the Father is like.

The more we know Him, the more we will know what love is really like. Jesus said that when we love Him—and lovingly obey Him---He and His Heavenly Father will make their home in us. John 14:23

That sounds like family.

HE WON'T FAIL YOU

Often, teachers naturally gravitate towards the more promising students---the motivated ones with good attitudes. It's easier to develop relationships with this kind of student, and sometimes the ones most apt to fail receive less attention.

Jesus usually does things differently than we would. One of the most revealing conversations recorded in the Bible was between Jesus and a Samaritan woman.

This woman had "FAILURE" written all over her. She had had five husbands and the man she was with now----well, she didn't even bother to get married.

She knew her "rank" and status in society; she was a Samaritan (not respected group) and she was a woman. (low status in that culture) So she was surprised that Jesus would ask her for a drink. Jesus seems to like to "lower our defenses" by His surprising ways.

Next, He used metaphors to pique her curiosity and open her mind to the possibility of a different kind of living. She didn't think He had the credentials to propose such a promise, and tried to dismiss what He said.

He assured her that He did, by exposing her need----and demonstrating how well He knew what she had been doing with her life.

Yet she still had some pride in her religious beliefs, and tried to discount what He was telling her and postpone the reckoning. His next words were like a bomb that blew away all her religious talk and cover-up. In the most direct way, He openly told her who He was: the Messiah. Now there could be no more pretenses.

She believed in Him-----enough to gather her whole village to hear Him. They listened to Jesus too, and believed. I don't think this woman was a failure anymore, after she began to live for Eternity's goals.

She had tasted the Living Water.

Do you want some? It's freely offered to you, no matter what kind of failure you have been. He doesn't look down on you.

Teachers, give your students some of the Living Water every day----this water brings Hope! Don't let the enemy brand some students as failures----even if they seem to be failing now. Go out of your way to give them a drink from the only well that truly satisfies.

This story of hope can be found in the Gospel of John, chapter 4.

HIS HEART

I have been thinking more about the Lord's heart----it is so great. There is no end to His capacity to care.

When you are around heartless people, it can wear away at your soul and make you forget the greatness of the Lord's heart.

I read this passage recently, and noticed especially what Jesus felt. Luke 7:11-13

"Soon afterward, Jesus went to a town called Nain, and his disciples and a large crowd went along with him. As he approached the town gate, a dead person was being carried out—the only son of his mother, and she was a widow. And a large crowd from the town was with her. When the Lord saw her, his heart went out to her and he said, "Don't cry.""

Why would He say, "Don't cry"? I don't think He is against expressing emotion. I don't think He was reprimanding her. I think her grief broke His heart.

His compassion for us is so great that not only did He die on the cross to pay the penalty for our sins, but He also bore our griefs and sorrows to the Cross.

"Surely He has borne our griefs
And carried our sorrows;
Yet we esteemed Him stricken,
Smitten by God, and afflicted."

Isaiah 53:4 NKJV

Our grief breaks His heart so much that He went to the Cross to end our sorrow.

We will not see the completion of this until He comes again.

Until then, we have His promise of His comfort from the Holy Spirit, and the strength of His presence. "I will never leave you; I will never abandon you." Hebrews 13:5 GNT

"I have told you these things, so that in me you may have peace. In this world you will have trouble. But take heart! I have overcome the world." John 16:33

Take heart! Be encouraged through His great heart.

He has never-ending compassion for you.

IDENTITY CRISIS

I am sure you have heard of the "coat of many colors". It has become something of an icon for the person of Joseph, whose story is told in Genesis.

That coat represented Joseph's identity in his father's household. It stood for prestige and privilege, the favor and blessing of his father, and his role of leader as his father's son.

The enemy of all that is good, prompted Joseph's brothers into following his evil plan. When they stripped away his colorful coat, in effect they stole his identity, killed his relationships, and destroyed his future role.

These are the tactics of the enemy: he comes to steal our identity as a believer, kill our relationships with the Lord and others, and destroy our work for the Kingdom of God. He wants to incapacitate us, and render us useless.

However, that coat of colors was not all that Joseph was. In the pit, as a slave, and in prison, Joseph's "true colors" showed. In his heart, he was a servant of God, and the Lord was with him. He was not abandoned by God, even though his brothers thought Joseph did not deserve to have the Presence of God.

Joseph was the prophetic one in the family, but his brothers didn't understand this and they despised him for it. The enemy knew the significance however; by removing the prophetic, he would encounter fewer obstacles to his plan of destroying the rest of the family. This family was special;

they were the descendants of Abraham, to whom had been given the promise of blessing the world.

The enemy wanted to stop this family from blessing anyone! But his plans often have a way of backfiring on him; instead of destroying the family through this evil deed, it became the means God used to rescue this family.

Through a strange course of events that fulfilled prophecy, Joseph saved his entire family from extinction. Years later, it was through this family that our Savior was born.

Who you really are is based on your relationship with the One who knows you thoroughly and loves you eternally---- Jesus. Be aware that there is also an enemy who will try to steal, kill, and destroy your influence. Overpower his plans with diligent prayer.

Every person you influence through your faith in the goodness of the Lord, may be used by the Lord to save his or her family. Our message is how valuable they are to the Lord, and how He wants to be with them, as He was with Joseph. It is the Lord's presence with us that makes us an influence on the world, as Joseph was.

EXCHANGE

What happens when you don't value truth? You exchange the truth for a lie.

It happened in the Garden of Eden. An outside influence made them value desire over truth and they bought the lie.

What happens when truth is exchanged---or bartered away---for a lie? Perversion. Romans 1:25-32.

The verb pervert means to corrupt, to profane, to demoralize, to poison or infect, to incite to evil, to ruin utterly in character or quality.

It also means: to distort the meaning of something in order to mislead, or to change the inherent purpose or function of something. Perversion is deliberately false in order to devalue and degrade.

What a terrible recompense for trading away truth!

"Buy the truth and do not sell it" Proverbs 23:23

When you exchange the truth for a lie, you are selling yourself into slavery and bondage.

Hold on to Truth!

ACCEPTED

Some people were disappointed in Jesus, because He wasn't what they expected.

He was rejected by society, had no prestige, and didn't fit in anywhere.

He didn't meet Judas' expectations, and you know what happened; Judas went to the religious rulers to betray Jesus.

Later Judas was remorseful that he had betrayed an innocent man---was that all he ever thought of Jesus?

Judas trusted the religious system of society more than in Jesus, but they in turn reviled him---they were untrustworthy.

When I finally saw myself as a sinner at the age of seventeen---and all illusions of "goodness" were gone, I had no expectations that Jesus would want me.

The fact that He did, makes me love Him so much---He loves a loser like me.

Yes, I was a bona fide loser.

I was losing confidence.

I was losing hope.

I was losing strength.

I was losing courage.

I was losing love.

I was losing joy.

I was losing satisfaction.

I was losing peace.

My life was on a downward spiral into negativity and loss every day. I was drowning in my own defeat and could not help myself.

"He reached down from on high and took hold of me; he drew me out of deep waters." Psalm 18:16

"He lifted me out of the slimy pit, out of the mud and mire; he set my feet on a rock and gave me a firm place to stand." Psalm 40:2

He rescued me; He IS my rock.

"The Lord is my rock, my fortress and my deliverer; my God is my rock, in whom I take refuge," Psalm 18:2

He will rescue you, too---and you will find that His mercy and love exceeds all expectations we could ever have.

HIS GLORY

This world has conditioned us to the normalcy of contempt towards people, and constant criticism. These things are not normal in the Kingdom of God; they don't belong in it.

It's amazing and refreshing to our souls to realize there is no contempt in Jesus! He will not leave you unchanged, or a captive to sin, but He does not treat us with contempt.

This is because contempt comes from self-righteousness and pride. Jesus doesn't have those either. People try to change others by using contempt, but it doesn't work. Jesus changes us by letting us see who He really is. He is real righteousness.

As we look into the mirror of His Word, we see Jesus and His reflection. The more we see Him the more we are changed, from "glory to glory".

"And we all, who with unveiled faces contemplate the Lord's glory, are being transformed into his image with ever-increasing glory, which comes from the Lord, who is the Spirit." 2 Corinthians 3:18

Seek the Lord and His glory! The more we have of Jesus inside, the more the world will see Him, too.

Cling to what is good---that is Jesus! Represent His goodness in a world full of evil.

HOLINESS

What exactly is it?

When the Lord says, "Be holy as I am holy"-----what exactly does He mean?

I think I am getting a better understanding.

Holiness is more than adherence to God's standards of morality. Holiness is more than our worship or a life of service to God.

Holiness is God's character. He wants to develop His character in us.

I Corinthians 13 is a picture of His character. This is the chapter that long ago showed me my sin nature, and how much I needed to be saved from it. I saw the holiness of God when I read it, and I wanted to be made new.

Religious practices or rituals can't make us holy, or make us new persons. Only the Holy Spirit can do that.

Holiness = living in God's love, motivated by His Holy Spirit.

The Old Testament laws are fulfilled in Christ---that means we can see the meaning of the Ten Commandments in Christ. They are all about loving God with all your heart and loving others with His love----treating other people as He would---with mercy and compassion and kindness.

His love is never lenient on sin, because sin is harmful and destroys people. He is intent on giving His help to rescue people.

"Without holiness, no one will see the Lord." Hebrews 12:14 No one will be able to see what the Lord is like, if we do not exhibit His character.

When Jesus looks at us, He looks beyond our faults and sees our needs. He gives us His grace to help us in our time of need. That is how we should look at others also---with His perception. That is holiness.

"Therefore, as God's chosen people, holy and dearly loved, clothe yourselves with compassion, kindness, humility, gentleness and patience. Bear with each other and forgive one another if any of you has a grievance against someone. Forgive as the Lord forgave you." Colossians 3:12-13

His love is holy, yet we can experience it!

In Heaven, we will breathe an atmosphere of His pure, Holy love, untainted by anything from the old sin nature that has caused so much pain.

Thank you, Jesus.

WHAT SIDE?

Jesus said that whoever is on the side of truth listens to Him. John 18:37

I think we could also deduce that whoever listens to Him, is on the side of truth.

About 80 times, Jesus prefaced His words with the statement, "I tell you the truth". I think it is very clear that if we don't know Jesus, we won't know the truth.

How important is truth? The only thing that can set people free is truth. John 8:32 We have no freedom without it.

There is an eternal guarantee on the truth of God's Word. He validates it, confirms it, it has gone through "quality testing", and it will never be voided or rescinded.

It cannot be contested in court, because He is the highest authority.

"so is my word that goes out from my mouth: It will not return to me empty, but will accomplish what I desire and achieve the purpose for which I sent it." Isaiah 55:11

"Your word, Lord, is eternal; it stands firm in the heavens." Psalm 119:89

"Your promises have been thoroughly tested, and your servant loves them." Psalm 119:140

"Heaven and earth will pass away, but my words will never pass away." Matthew 24:35

Stay on the side of Truth----His truth will win in the end.

FREEDOM

When there is a warning in Scripture, we should pay attention. We are in danger if we do not heed His voice. This is not a life of condemnation; that is not the reason for the warning.

We are as helpless as sheep if we don't listen to His voice--- the Good Shepherd's voice. Walk in the light, and follow Him.

"But if we walk in the light, as he is in the light, we have fellowship with one another, and the blood of Jesus, his Son, purifies us from all sin." I John 1:7

This is meant to be a life free from bondages of sin. The more we seek Him, the more freedom we find. We must not let the things of God become routine---it's not a religious business or a social club. "walk in newness of life." Romans 6:4 NKJV

It would be hard to trust the love of someone you thought only wanted to reproach you and condemn you. The Lord wants to help us. We have to receive His help; human willpower cannot defeat the nature of sin, in or by itself. If we don't seek the Lord and cling to His promises, the old sin nature will try to take over. So He warns us of these things.

If we think of the Lord as a treacherous tyrant, we won't be able to trust Him. We have to trust His love and be convinced of His good character. We must fear to disobey Him because of the dangerous consequences, but always trust His goodness. That kind of "fear" is respect for Him, not a cringing dread.

It is the nature of Satan to accuse and condemn. It is the nature of Jesus to heal and restore. He began His ministry with the proclamation found in Isaiah 61:1-2

"The Spirit of the Sovereign Lord is on me, because the Lord has anointed me to proclaim good news to the poor. He has sent me to bind up the brokenhearted, to proclaim freedom for the captives and release from darkness for the prisoners, to proclaim the year of the LORD's favor…"

I have discovered another paradox: You cannot find this freedom from bondage unless you surrender yourself completely and irrevocably, without reserve, to the Lord.

Yet He is nothing like the person who offers only conditional love---the person who gives "love" only when you allow them to dominate you and control you---and who withholds "love" until you flatter, appease, and cater to them.

The world's culture says in effect, "I won't love you unless you let me squeeze you into my mold." But where the Spirit of the Lord is, there is freedom!! 2 Corinthians 3:17

The Lord's reign and rule over us sets us free to be who He designed us to be----not what others think we should be.

Don't let anything take away your faith in Him!! It is our victory.

"for everyone born of God overcomes the world. This is the victory that has overcome the world, even our faith."
1 John 5:4

TRUST

Many people have a fear of being vulnerable. They become critical and put others down because of their own insecurities. It's a reaction to our "me-first", "dog-eat-dog" competitive, comparing world.

They build a wall around themselves based on their own opinions---establishing in their minds that no one is right but them---to protect themselves from the fear of being wrong or inadequate.

They frequently change their viewpoint and adapt their opinions to whatever will protect them the most.....to be on whatever looks like the winning side.

They stubbornly convince themselves that no one can tear down that wall.

There is One who can......Jesus......nothing is impossible for Him. He specializes in this.

We can't truly follow Jesus until we lose this self-reliance and this habit of self-protection. He wants to take us far beyond our own opinions into living in His supernatural ways.

You lose yourself and then actually find yourself—the Real You---when you put your trust in Jesus and He becomes your security.

He will not use you for His "game plan" and then discard you for something more advantageous. He will not exploit your heart with His demands, and then leave you alone and disillusioned.

Our perceptions of Him are affected by our human culture, and we have to slowly learn to "see" how different His nature is from ours.

I think this is what Romans 12:2 means to us:

"Do not conform to the pattern of this world, but be transformed by the renewing of your mind. Then you will be able to test and approve what God's will is—his good, pleasing and perfect will."

His response to our need is not emotional blackmail---He does not withhold His love when He is displeased. If we seek Him, we will find Him. If we draw near to Him, He responds with His grace, mercy, and help.

It is His presence that transforms us….to be like Him. And that is our destiny.

"Trust in the LORD with all your heart and lean not on your own understanding; in all your ways submit to him, and he will make your paths straight." Proverbs 3:5-6

THE HOPE OF ABRAHAM

We have the advantage of seeing the outcome of Abraham's life—and that God did give him and Sarah a child.

But what if we had lived in Abraham's lifetime---if we had been Abraham's friends before Isaac was born, how would we have reacted?

When you are in the years of waiting for a promise to be fulfilled, people can get tired of what looks like an "unreasonable attitude" to them.

And so I think that Abraham's waiting for a child must have become tiresome to other people. They probably thought he was being obstinate, holding on to something that looked like false hope. His friends must have wanted to say to him, "Why can't you let go of this idea and move on with your life---and accept things the way they are?" Maybe they even accused him of being "in denial" of the reality of Sarah's age. Her child bearing years were long gone.

Faith can look foolish, frivolous, irrational, and even arrogant. Yet Abraham chose to look delusional rather than to show a lack of trust in the One he followed.

His confidence about himself, his life, and his joy all came from his relationship with this One who had spoken to him.

But to disbelieve the promise that was given to him would be to dishonor the integrity and character of the God who had revealed Himself to him.

It would be distrust of this God who had called to him by name.

He couldn't do it---he could not prefer the opinions of other people over the truthfulness of the Lord, who had showed His love to him in an intimate way.

He could not betray that trust.

So he held on to his hope in spite of his age, in spite of the impossibilities, in spite of what others thought.

And God answered.

He proved that His Word endures.

He fulfills all His promises---no matter how impossible it seems.

Let go of the past----but hold on to your future.

Put your hope in God's Word.

"May those who fear you rejoice when they see me, for I have put my hope in your word." Psalm 119:74

UNDER CONSTRUCTION

Society is always putting up barriers to exclude people, whether visible or invisible. I am sure you have heard those voices---"You don't fit in", "You don't belong here", "You embarrass us", "You are out of style", "You are not clever enough", "You don't measure up to our standards".

One thing I am still realizing about Jesus is that He likes to tear barriers down.

In nursery class, when we taught about Joshua and the battle of Jericho, we used to let the children build a wall of cardboard bricks, and knock it down with beach balls. I think Jesus enjoys knocking down walls, too.

The biggest barrier He knocked down was the wall of sin separating us from our Heavenly Father. When Jesus died, and the Temple curtain ripped from top to bottom, it was a victory statement.

He paid the ultimate price to bring that barrier down.

The apostle Paul found out that it was Jesus' plan to knock down the wall separating the Jews and Gentiles, through faith in Him. (Ephesians 2:14-16.)

Jesus is still in construction---He is building us into a habitation for His presence.

"In him the whole building is joined together and rises to become a holy temple in the Lord. And in him you too are being built together to become a dwelling in which God lives by his Spirit." Ephesians 2:21-22

In the Lord's house, there aren't supposed to be any barriers----no distinctions between race, social status, economic level, etc. (Galatians 3:28) The building can't grow with all those limitations.

There should however, be a barrier to sin and evil. What God says is sinful, remains so. He does not change His declaration, regardless of how society changes its opinions.

1 Corinthians 6:9, 1 Timothy 1:9-11, Romans 1:26-27

We are the living stones He uses for this holy temple---and each one of us is necessary and has a place where we fit into the building.

"As you come to him, the living Stone—rejected by humans but chosen by God and precious to him— you also, like living stones, are being built into a spiritual house to be a holy priesthood, offering spiritual sacrifices acceptable to God through Jesus Christ." 1 Peter 2:4-5

If He is going to "enlarge" us so that He can use us more to build His house, He just might have to knock down some walls.

TRUE SUCCESS

Lately, there is a human characteristic that I am noticing with great abhorrence: Scorn. I see it everywhere in the world system, in society and its mores, in the Pharisees…. and sadly, sometimes in myself.

I think success is a god that we instinctively run after without realizing it…and scorn is society's weapon to punish those who do not have it. And though we deplore this, some small part of us may be secretly pleased when others fail, if it makes us feel more successful.

I don't see any scorn at all in Jesus. He had no scorn for the woman who had five husbands and a lover; he had no scorn for the woman caught in the very act of adultery; he had no scorn for Peter even after he cursed and denied he knew Jesus.

Instead, He loved these people and desired a relationship with them. He wanted to help them, not condemn them. Yet He did this without condoning their sin---He intended to provide the way for freedom from every sin that threatens to control our lives and dictate our destinies.

Our nature is so opposite from His that we can't even comprehend the difference or even recognize it at times.

"For my thoughts are not your thoughts, neither are your ways my ways," declares the Lord. "As the heavens are higher than the earth, so are my ways higher than your ways and my thoughts than your thoughts." Isaiah 55:8-9

Scorn and desire for success are so ingrained in us that we don't even suspect that they are totally unnatural for Jesus. In Isaiah 53, we can see the qualities of His nature. Lord, open our eyes to see You and marvel.

When He was a carpenter here on earth, I don't think He would have ever done shabby work. However, I think that He was content and satisfied in this occupation and status during that time.

"Who, being in very nature God, did not consider equality with God something to be used to his own advantage; rather, he made himself nothing by taking the very nature of a servant, being made in human likeness." Philippians 2:6-7

Whenever we stoop to using worldly methods to achieve "success" in spiritual matters, I am sure we offend the Holy Spirit, and inadvertently defeat ourselves. We are helpless and foolish, ignorant and senseless without the guidance of the Holy Spirit. How we need Him!

I think true success is when we become everything He ever wanted us to be. Only His purposes and His anointing give our lives significance.

"As for me, I will be vindicated and will see your face; when I awake, I will be satisfied with seeing your likeness." Psalm 17:15

"Dear friends, now we are children of God, and what we will be has not yet been made known. But we know that when Christ appears, we shall be like him, for we shall see him as he is. All who have this hope in him purify themselves, just as he is pure." 1 John 3:2-3

ISSUES

She was bleeding....her life and strength was slowly leaving her. Not only that, she was alone. No one wanted to have anything to do with her because of this affliction.

She felt she was under a curse, and no one cared. Friends deserted her, thinking she was not fit for friendship or fellowship anymore.

She had an unresolved issue---an agony of pain and isolation that would not go away, no matter what she tried.

She heard of a man who had power to heal with God's love, and a very tiny hope began to grow. One day there was a crowd in the street---they were following Him.

That hope grew into courage that moved her feet to follow her heart. But she found that she was like a ghost----no one knew she was there, and they did not make room for her to get close to Him.

It was as if she no longer existed except in some faint memory from long ago.

But His voice drew her....she determined to press through the hindering attitudes of the people around her who gave her no thought at all.

She pushed a way through the self-absorbed people who thought she deserved no notice....or any place among them. Like a ghost, no one was aware of her.

But He felt her touch.

She had grabbed hold of the hem of His garment, and power flowed from Him into her body. She was healed; she knew that the bleeding had stopped.

But then He drew attention to her; she could not escape the way she came. He caused everyone to notice what she did. She was trembling but she came to Him and knelt at His feet. And then He praised her in front of everyone.

He gave her the highest acclamation possible; He commended her faith. And He named her as one of His family; He called her His daughter.

He healed her shame and exclusion and gave her the gift of His peace. And her story continues to be told, recorded in Luke 8:43-48.

Her faith shows us an example to follow.

Don't give in to discouragement, hopelessness, and apathy. Don't back down to spirits of exclusion, rejection, and condemnation.

Press through these hindering attitudes, and touch Jesus. Kneel at His feet and worship Him with passion! Bless Him with your faith.

"Resist the devil, and he will flee from you." James 4:7 This resistance is not a passive half-hearted action; this is an all-out effort.

Resist the enemy by fervent prayer and passionate worship. Forget who is around you and what they will think about you, and press through to touch Jesus.

You will never regret it.

BATTLE STRATEGIES

I admit it.

I have a defective, disabled, devitalized personality.

But when my living room becomes a war room, something happens. I exchange my poor personality for the Holy Spirit's personality, and He gives me His dynamics!

"But You, O Lord, are a shield for me, My glory and the One who lifts up my head." Psalm 3:3 NKJV

The enemy's net that held me down mentally is thrown off, and I have the Lord's confidence.

"With your help I can advance against a troop; with my God I can scale a wall." Psalm 18:29

"He trains my hands for battle; my arms can bend a bow of bronze." Psalm 18:34

We become part of His strategy when we pray in the "War Room"! The Holy Spirit can go places we can't go; He can go right into the hub of the enemy's stronghold, and right into the hearts of those who are enslaved to evil.

"The weapons we fight with are not the weapons of the world. On the contrary, they have divine power to demolish strongholds." 2 Corinthians 10:4

The Lord reminded me again, that we are not fighting people; we are fighting the spirits that are controlling or affecting them.

"For our struggle is not against flesh and blood, but against the rulers, against the authorities, against the powers of this dark world and against the spiritual forces of evil in the heavenly realms." Ephesians 6:12

I am convinced that the lust for dominance, rule, and control, combined with a false religious zeal, is the force motivating all the terrorism and violence. Strike that spirit of lust with prayer.

"You, dear children, are from God and have overcome them, because the one who is in you is greater than the one who is in the world." I John 4:4 There is no power greater than the Lord's power and authority.

I see that the enemy is targeting colleges and schools with his lies; so we need to target these areas in our nation with offensive prayer.

Nothing can stand against Holy Spirit led prayer.

A SPACE PARABLE

We believe in the existence of cyberspace, even though we can't see it; it is just as logical to believe in the spiritual realm. Things are constantly happening all around us that we cannot see with our eyes.

Even physical things are not as solid as they appear. They are actually made of tiny bits of matter called molecules, which are held together by what most scientists explain as "chemical bonds". The complete answer is Jesus.

"He is the sole expression of the glory of God [the Light being, the out-raying or radiance of the divine], and He is the perfect imprint and very image of [God's] nature, upholding and maintaining and guiding and propelling the universe by His mighty word of power." Heb. 1:3 AMPC

That is incredible power! His Word holds the universe together! And we have access to all the "updates" in this powerful Word of God.

Regular and daily updates are vital to protect our minds from the "spiritual" viruses waiting to implant themselves in our minds and corrupt its files.

God's Word is the perfect virus protection---it catches anything and everything, and can clean whatever viruses may have attached to us.

Updates are essential to prevent sluggishness, and to have full operating capacity.

"Do not conform to the pattern of this world, but be transformed by the renewing of your mind. Then you will be able to test and approve what God's will is---his good, pleasing and perfect will." Romans 12:2.

"But his delight and desire are in the law of the Lord, and on His law (the precepts, the instructions, the teachings of God) he habitually meditates (ponders and studies) by day and by night." Psalm 1:2 AMPC

We need the Holy Spirit to refresh us, through worship, to eliminate faulty connections.

We might need to restore ourselves to a previous time, through seeking the Lord in prayer, to get rid of any troublesome downloads or glitches in the system.

Let Jesus be the Lord of your "cyberspace".

VALUES

How much are you worth? I cringe inside when I have to list material assets to determine "net worth". It doesn't make me feel very valuable! But it makes me grateful that I don't live by those standards.

I'm always relieved to hear what Jesus said in Luke 12:15--- "life does not consist in an abundance of possessions."

In the world, the value of people fluctuates according to their popularity, wealth, looks, and accomplishments. In God's Kingdom, however, the value of people never fluctuates or diminishes. They have intrinsic worth, which is established by God. And there is no depreciation scale.

He set their value when He gave something of infinite and extraordinary worth to purchase their freedom from sin's tyranny; the blood of His Son, Jesus. 1 Peter 1:18-20

The world screams at us that we are inferior, unattractive, undesirable, ignorant, insignificant, useless, and unwanted. Ironically, the deepest need of people in this world is to be accepted, loved and valued.

Jesus came into this world to tell us that He wants us, cherishes us, delights in us, has a purpose for us, and includes us------and He proved it all by dying for us. Always believe in His love for you, no matter what happens.

"This is love: not that we loved God, but that he loved us and sent his Son as an atoning sacrifice for our sins." 1 John 4:10 The blood of Jesus will never lose its eternal value--- and neither will you, if you belong to Him.

PAY IT FORWARD

The penalty for your sins has already been paid.

Jesus paid it forward about 2000 years ago.

We don't deserve it, can't in any way pay it back, and can't ever merit it at all---but Take the Gift of salvation!!

He wants you to have it.

It's an outrageously generous act of mercy from the One whose heart is as big as the universe. Don't refuse His gift!

Now, it's your turn----pay it forward. Share the gift---show His forgiveness. Demonstrate His kindness and compassion.

Be patient with others----and especially with children. Be gentle with others---and especially with children.

In a world full of bad news, share the Good News of His story often---and especially to children.

"Grace and peace to you from God our Father and the Lord Jesus Christ, who gave himself for our sins to rescue us from the present evil age, according to the will of our God and Father," Galatians 1:3-4

"And let us consider how we may spur one another on toward love and good deeds," Hebrews 10:24

WALKWAYS

"Do two walk together unless they have agreed to do so?"
Amos 3:3

If we agree with Jesus and what He says through the Holy
Spirit, we will find ourselves on His walkway---and going in
His direction.

This kind of agreement is more than a mental assent---it is
more like a contract or a firm commitment.

If we don't have that kind of relationship with Jesus in which
we continually pledge our lives to Him, we will soon discover
that we are going a different direction---and on a different
path than Him.

If we are not in agreement with His Word to obey it, we are
breaking our covenant with Him.

The only way to walk with Him---in the direction He is going--
is to agree with His Word wholeheartedly----and the result of
this agreement is obedience.

We are to walk in His ways---His "walkway". Psalm 119:3-4
He has laid down precepts that are to be fully obeyed.

What are His ways? Micah 6:8 tells us that His ways are: to
act justly, to love mercy, and to walk humbly with our God.

Walk humbly means to walk as a servant does, who is
obedient, attentive, submissive, and reverent---to the Holy
Spirit, who is our guide.

If the Holy Spirit convicts you of anything, don't resist Him---agree with Him quickly!

"This is the message we have heard from him and declare to you: God is light; in him there is no darkness at all.

If we claim to have fellowship with him and yet walk in the darkness, we lie and do not live out the truth.

But if we walk in the light, as he is in the light, we have fellowship with one another, and the blood of Jesus, his Son, purifies us from all sin.

If we claim to be without sin, we deceive ourselves and the truth is not in us.

If we confess our sins, he is faithful and just and will forgive us our sins and purify us from all unrighteousness"
1 John 1:5-9

This is how we continue to walk in His light. His walkway is full of light.

This is the blessing of His walkway!

God has no shadow. When we follow Jesus, we will not be walking in darkness.

"When Jesus spoke again to the people, he said, "I am the light of the world. Whoever follows me will never walk in darkness, but will have the light of life." John 8:12

This walkway is where we find our purpose.

PAWNED

When she walked in that day, she did not know that she would be a pawn. She would be the chess piece the players would move around in their strategy to outwit the opponent. She had no value to them beyond this, and no strategy of her own.

It took all of her faith just to come, since she was condemned in the eyes of most people who would be there.

She was stooped and bent over, and had learned to walk in her shame. No confidence would allow her to stand up straight now; she was crippled for life. And it had been that way for 18 years.

She could not even remember a time when things had been different---a time when she laughed and ran and played.

There was no going back; no rewind button---and going forward meant slowly shuffling one foot in front of the other, and looking down----always looking down.

Despite all this, the enemy of her soul could not take away her most prized possession: her faith. Whatever happened to her in this life, she knew that God was good. And so she came to His house without fail through her painful shuffling.

Once she was there she knew she would endure the scornful looks of those who had no knowledge of pain, and the pitiful response of those who looked away from her.

Today something was different; there was someone there who was different from all the others. She was drawn to raise her eyes and look into his----what was it that she saw in them? Could it be-----admiration? For her?

What would he find to admire in a stooped bent-over woman? No, it could not be---the flicker of light vanished from her mind.

She was crippled, and she was not even sure why. Some said it was due to her sin, others said it was lack of faith, and some said it was because of a curse on her family.

She forgave their ignorance, since she herself did not understand why she could not stand up.

Then this Man called her to come forward, and though she did not know the reason, she did as he said. The synagogue ruler watched her as she shuffled her way to the front.

The Man said to her, "Woman, you are set free from your infirmity." Then he put his hands on her, and immediately her back began to straighten!

She lost all reserve then, and burst out into praise to God.

Then she saw the disgust on the ruler's face---and noticed the cold, displeased stare he gave the Man. The rule had been broken, and the ruler was indignant. "There are six days for work. So come and be healed on those days, not on the Sabbath," he told all the people.

Suddenly, she realized who this synagogue ruler was---and other men like him. They were Fault-Finders; people who live to criticize and punish anyone they perceive as a threat.

They did not know God as He really is: a Healer and Restorer because of His great compassion. And she realized that not only was her body crippled, but her mind had been crippled by the attitude of such men. They did not care whether she could walk straight or not; they wanted to use this incident to show disfavor to this Man. To them, she was only a pawn.

But to the Healer, she was far more. He answered the ruler by saying, "You hypocrites! Doesn't each of you on the Sabbath untie his ox or donkey from the stall and lead it out to give it water? Then should not this woman, a daughter of Abraham, whom Satan has kept bound for eighteen long years, be set free on the Sabbath day from what bound her?"

At this, the Healer's opponents were humiliated, but the people there who saw the wonderful thing that had happened, were delighted. The woman was standing up perfectly straight---and she was standing with a confidence they had never before seen in her.

Not only did this Man heal her body and cause her to stand up straight, but He then stood up for her! She felt as though a huge burden fell off of her back. It was not her fault! She was not to blame for her infirmity!

The One who had the authority to heal said so----he put the blame on Satan. He did not think of her as a sinner, or a cursed person---he called her a daughter of Abraham. In her culture, that was the highest of honors.

Abraham was known as the father of faith----to be considered his daughter meant that you indeed had displayed great faith.

And it meant that she was a friend of God. He stood up for her, and now she was able to stand.

This story is found in Luke 13:10-17.

DISCONTENT

How did he do it? How did this evil creature seduce the first two humans into doing exactly what God said not to do?

They were surrounded by the beauty of a perfect world---an expression of God's goodness to them.

They had no discomfort of any kind whatsoever---and no lack of anything they needed.

And yet, this monster was successful.

The enemy plotted against these two children of God, but he could not get to them or harm them------until he was able to make Eve discontent.

The enemy began to imply that God was denying them something through His commands. It began the age-old question concerning submission to God: "What's in it for me?"

So you can see that discontent with God's commands is the "oldest trick in the book."

I have heard some say, "I tried prayer and it didn't work." Or, "If God is talking to me, I sure don't hear Him."

I think that these are excuses to cover up that the heart wants its own way.

Satan plots against us to use our sensual and natural desires to deceive us. He created a desire in Eve for selfish ambition through discontent-----to be *as* God, instead of maintaining a dependency upon God.

73

Satan made God's character look "bad" to Eve---as if the Lord was depriving them of pleasure by withholding the fruit of that tree from them.

And the secular world still condemns God's character and blames Him for withholding from us and denying us the pleasure of our own way.

Discontent will drive us to deny what is true.
Discontent will drive us to disobey.
Discontent will drive us to follow our own desires, instead of the Lord's desires.

And chaos is the result.

Independence from God does not lead to freedom. Instead, we become subject to the tyranny of another---our sinful selves, which can be easily deceived and manipulated by the enemy of our souls. JESUS CAME TO RESCUE US!!

Unless He rules our hearts, we are never free. We will always be slaves to sin, and its consequences.

In whatever circumstances we find ourselves, Lord help us remember Your goodness and Your love for us.

Remind us that Your plans are for good, and not for evil. Help us not to complain, but to trust.

Contentment in Your love is the greatest security we could ever have.

I pray that America will repent of flaunting the evil of independence from God's rule, and will once again promote the freedom that comes with dependence upon God.

DAVID'S LEGACY

He became a hero…then a legend…then the king. He was well-renowned, well-respected, and well-liked.

Then suddenly one day he was none of those things.

He had to leave the palace and run for his life….again. This time, the threat was not a king who was jealous of his fame as a warrior. It was his own son, Absalom, who turned against him and turned many people against him.

Since it had been many years since his warrior feats, David was not popular anymore with the young and the restless.

Wisdom and experience meant little to them, and they were tired of his rule. Absalom had ambition and initiative, and quickly gained a following.

The opinions of people are not to be trusted; they can be easily manipulated. It's part of the downfall of human nature; we are easily duped and follow each other like sheep.

This is why we need a shepherd who is not affected by change. We need a foundation that is not under pressure to conform. We need a gardener who is not subject to whims, and will cultivate us faithfully.

We need Jesus.

We need Him to be in charge of our lives. He is the one unbiased Authority who will never desert you, fail you, or think of you differently as time goes on.

His love for you is unchanging.

He is steadfast, reliable, and completely trustworthy. He keeps every one of His promises; He always has, and He always will. There is no one else like this.

Plots and intrigues should not be a part of the Kingdom of God, but sadly, they are when people forget that the Lord's Kingdom is not part of this world.

It happens when people who belong to Jesus forget they are citizens of Heaven, and they begin to act like people whose hope is only in this world.

That is when they grapple and grasp at positions of authority, and push and shove others out of the way.

David's legacy was not an earthly kingdom. His legacy was his faith in the Lord, and that is for all of us.

Absalom's passion was not in Heavenly things, and he lost the legacy....and his life.

David's legacy has been passed down to us through his heir: the Messiah. Through Jesus, we have inherited the promises of God made to David. We are the heirs of Jesus.

He is our true King, and His kingdom will never end.

"He will be great and will be called the Son of the Most High. The Lord God will give him the throne of his father David, and he will reign over Jacob's descendants forever; his kingdom will never end." Luke 1:32-33

LET IT GO

There's a popular song that urges one to "let it go". But the theme of the song is not about the motto, "Let go and let God". The lyrics are really more about casting off restraints, rather than releasing something for the greater good.

I've been thinking about that issue: When do we let go----and when do we hold on?

The question is really WHAT do we let go?

God's Word always has the right answers.

We have to let go of the past, because it can't be changed.

"But one thing I do: Forgetting what is behind and straining toward what is ahead, I press on toward the goal to win the prize for which God has called me heavenward in Christ Jesus." Philippians 3:13-14

We must let go of bitterness and resentment because these things hurt us.

"Get rid of all bitterness, rage and anger, brawling and slander, along with every form of malice." Ephesians 4:31

We need to let go of things that hinder our progress in spiritual maturity.

"Therefore, since we are surrounded by such a great cloud of witnesses, let us throw off everything that hinders and the sin that so easily entangles. And let us run with perseverance the race marked out for us," Hebrews 12:1

I think these are some of the things that hinder and weigh us down: discouragement, fear, depression, worry, and self-pity. One of the sins that can easily entangle us here in America is greed. Our nation is obsessed with pleasures and possessions.

I found one more thing: Let go of anything false---false teachings or ideas.

"Nevertheless, I have a few things against you: There are some among you who hold to the teaching of Balaam, who taught Balak to entice the Israelites to sin so that they ate food sacrificed to idols and committed sexual immorality. Likewise, you also have those who hold to the teaching of the Nicolaitans." Revelation 2:14-15

But I think the most strategic aspect of letting go is this: Let Your Self Go.

It's the leap of faith into a spiritual reality that you have never seen before---you don't know what it will be like because you can't experience it until you are willing to let go and JUMP---- until you are ready to give your life away to Someone you cannot even see.

Jesus said: "For whoever wants to save their life will lose it, but whoever loses their life for me will find it." Matthew 16:25

This is where the adventure begins---Hold on for the ride!!

DUNAMIS

Dunamis: the Greek word translated into English as power, potential, force, energy.

The energy unleashed when the Resurrection power of the Holy Spirit came into that dark tomb where Christ's body lay, some have likened to the power of an atomic bomb.

Remember that it was the Holy Spirit who was the agent at Creation. When God said "Let there be Light", it was the Holy Spirit who made it happen.

I imagine that there was an explosion of Light when the Holy Spirit raised Jesus from the dead. Darkness and Death fled the scene, when that Light burst from the tomb.

We as believers have that same Resurrection power of the Holy Spirit inside of us!

"And if the Spirit of him who raised Jesus from the dead is living in you, he who raised Christ from the dead will also give life to your mortal bodies because of his Spirit who lives in you." Romans 8:11

"I pray that the eyes of your heart may be enlightened in order that you may know the hope to which he has called you, the riches of his glorious inheritance in his holy people, and his incomparably great power for us who believe. That power is the same as the mighty strength he exerted when he raised Christ from the dead and seated him at his right hand in the heavenly realms," Ephesians 1:18-20

The enemy of course wants us to feel like a "dud"----like a fireworks piece that fizzles out.

We are not----we have just not discovered the "dunamis" within---the dynamite of the Holy Spirit!

The words dynamite and dynamic both come from the Greek word dunamis.

After the Resurrection, Jesus sent the Holy Spirit on the Day of Pentecost.

He unleashed the power that raised Him from the dead, into our lives!! We have not yet realized---or seen the reality---of the extent of this power----the potential of the Holy Spirit.

We will see it when revival fully comes----continue to pray for revival-----and hold on!

"After they prayed, the place where they were meeting was shaken. And they were all filled with the Holy Spirit and spoke the word of God boldly." Acts 4:31

Press through self-consciousness and self-absorption.

Press through timidity and insecurity.

Press through hurt, rejection, grief, and negative opinions into the anointing the Lord wants to give us through the power of the Holy Spirit. This is where LIFE is!!!

Resurrection power is real in His presence.

YOUR PLACE

We used to do an object lesson with a wooden heart that a craftsman had made. It had an empty part in the middle in the shape of a cross. Nothing would fit that space except the wooden cross that was made to fit inside this heart.

There is a place in our heart that only Jesus can fill. Without His presence there, we will always feel empty.

One day, I was feeling particularly left out....and the Lord spoke these things to my heart:

"YOU WILL NEVER BE LEFT OUT OF MY LOVE. THERE IS A PLACE FOR YOU IN MY HEART THAT ONLY YOU CAN FILL."

There is a place set for you at His table.....don't let it remain empty. Come and eat and fellowship with Him.

"People will come from east and west and north and south, and will take their places at the feast in the kingdom of God." Luke 13:29

"Here I am! I stand at the door and knock. If you hear my voice and open the door, I will come in and eat with you, and you will eat with me." Revelation 3:20 NCV

Don't lose your place.....respond to His voice.

DEATH

"The last enemy to be destroyed will be death."
1 Corinthians 15:26 NCV

A friend recently reminded me that the Lord does not waste our sorrows. He grows something beautiful out of our pain.

The Lord is described by Isaiah as a man acquainted with grief and sorrow. "He is despised and rejected by men, a Man of sorrows and acquainted with grief." Isaiah 53:3 NKJV

He did this for our sakes, so that He would experience everything that we go through in this life. (Hebrews 2:17-18)

He even experienced death for our sakes.

"But we do see Jesus, who was made lower than the angels for a little while, now crowned with glory and honor because he suffered death, so that by the grace of God he might taste death for everyone." Hebrews 2:9

He overcame Death! He came to destroy it.

"Since the children have flesh and blood, he too shared in their humanity so that by his death he might break the power of him who holds the power of death—that is, the devil—" Hebrews 2:14

We do not yet see the full completion of this, but it is in God's plans for the future. "He will wipe every tear from their eyes. There will be no more death or mourning or crying or pain, for the old order of things has passed away." Revelation 21:4

For now, we may still have grief. Jesus tells us: "I have told you all this so that you may have peace in me. Here on earth you will have many trials and sorrows. But take heart, because I have overcome the world." John 16:33 NLT

Jesus promised to send us His Holy Spirit to be our Comforter and Helper.

"And I will ask the Father, and He will give you another Comforter (Counselor, Helper, Intercessor, Advocate, Strengthener, and Standby), that He may remain with you forever---" John 14:16 AMPC

One way that the Holy Spirit comforts us is to remind us of all the promises that Jesus has given to us----promises of hope and a future. John 14:26, Jeremiah 29:11

"May the God of hope fill you with all joy and peace as you trust in him, so that you may overflow with hope by the power of the Holy Spirit." Romans 15:13

Some cultures have tried to glorify death; they try to make it seem a beautiful thing with poetic tributes, elaborate "after-life" tomb furnishings, and honor for those who die by choice.

Jesus never did that; He came to conquer death. He wept when His friend Lazarus died, even though He knew that He was going to raise Lazarus from the dead.

Death is still the enemy----but because of Christ, it is a defeated enemy. DEATH WILL END.

FOREVER YOUNG

One of the things that I really enjoyed about working with children is that you can be silly, crazy, and undignified, and get away with it!

Children enjoy joy, and the freedom of expressing it. Their hearts are not weighed down with the need to criticize others or compete in social hierarchies.

Some people are so bound up in themselves that this kind of freedom is foreign to them. I think it was so sad that David's wife Michal was disgusted with him for dancing in worship to the Lord. He knew that freedom to express joy, but she didn't. She was offended by it.

When children praise God, it is real. They haven't yet learned social skills of pretense, or covering up disdain. They respond easily to God's presence.

And Jesus loves their praise and worship. As Jesus came into Jerusalem riding on a donkey, the children were shouting "Hosanna" and praising the Lord.

The religious leaders hated it, and tried to force Jesus to make them stop. He refused---He said if they stopped, even the rocks would start praising God.

I think I would rather be like a child, and not like a rock that has to be forced into it!

When commended for it, children can develop a keen discernment for God's voice. I remember how awed I was when the Holy Spirit led our daughter Naomi to pray with her grandfather, and he accepted Jesus as his savior.

At ten years old, she went to his house next door, with her children's Bible, and clearly explained to him what he needed to do. A little more than a year after that, he went home to be with the Lord.

After being in a children's environment, sometimes being in an atmosphere of stuffy sophisticated ambition can be like a torture chamber! Thankfully, the Holy Spirit can change the attitudes in us and refresh us.

It has been years since Guy and I have been able to go to kids' camp, but that is one of the best experiences of our lives. There is nothing like it----the children's services are incredible. In their own environment like this, a large group of children are uninhibited in seeking God.

Their responses to the Holy Spirit are the most awesome thing to see. It will change you. I wish that every parent had a chance to witness this.

I know that sometimes it is a popular thing to talk about "freedom"---it's something of a trend in Christian "lingo"----but I can assure you, that is not the motivation for children to be that way. It's simply how they are, and Jesus prizes that quality. I do too.

It is possible to become that way again. You may be getting old on the outside, but you can have a childlike heart on the inside. With Jesus, you are forever young.

AWARDS

In the spring, I see all the pictures of awards, posted by very proud and happy parents. They take delight in their children, and in their accomplishments, progress, and character development.

It makes me think of the Father's pleasure in His children. You are not a clone, a robot, or just another human being. You are His unique creation—you are His child.

Since he is such a good Father, I know that He is extremely excited and interested in what we are doing, and how we are progressing. I want to make Him proud!

Don't live for people's opinions, live for His! "and find out what pleases the Lord." Ephesians 5:10

"Thou art worthy, O Lord, to receive glory and honour and power: for thou hast created all things, and for thy pleasure they are and were created." Revelations 4:11 KJV

We were created for His pleasure! We can give Him joy as our children (and grandchildren) do to us. He delights in us when we want to please Him. Psalm 147:11

Have you ever noticed how children walk like their parents? I have observed this many times---children unconsciously imitate the physical traits of their parents' walk.

"Imitate God, therefore, in everything you do, because you are his dear children. Live a life filled with love, following the example of Christ. He loved us and offered himself as a sacrifice for us, a pleasing aroma to God." Eph. 5:1-2 NLT

Like your children imitate the way you walk, imitate your loving Father, and the way He walks. "walk by the Spirit, and you will not gratify the desires of the flesh." Galatians 5:16

Whose desires will be gratified? God's will---that is why He gives us His Holy Spirit---to make it possible for us to please Him. Hebrews 11:6 shows us:

1) That He is real

2) That it is possible to please Him through faith

3) He rewards us for seeking Him earnestly---we can have a relationship with Him.

4) He is appreciative---His character is trustworthy.

There are some who think of Him as a cold-hearted Being who only punishes, and has no regard for people. To others, He looks like a hateful person who only exists to deny them what they want.

The human sinful nature, with its lusts and desires, wars against God's holy nature, and the enemy of our souls always tries to make us mistrust the character of God.

But He is our Father. If there were some evil force in the world that was threatening to destroy your children, wouldn't you hate that evil? That is why God hates sin---it will destroy us if it is not dealt with. His desire is to save us---not to let us be destroyed.

He loves us with all His heart, and that is bigger than the universe.

Make Him proud!!

GET OUT OF DEFAULT

It is getting ridiculous; now someone decided they won't celebrate Valentine's Day because it might be offensive.

The nature of the world's culture is easily offended; in fact, the default position seems to be, "I am offended"--- to protest the differences it does not accept....or just to exercise control.

It's a manifestation of the lust for control that is inherent in our culture.

It's a form of the "It's all about ME, and what I want, and you don't matter" attitude.

The ones with the most power get to make the rules.

Among the people of God, it should be the opposite; appreciation of each other should be the norm.

God does not make clones; He makes unique individuals, and we are all special to Him.

Communist governments thought unity meant uniformity; everyone had to dress alike, think alike, and talk alike. This was a means to control people; that kind of "unity" is false.

God's people are the body of Christ. Just as in the human body, every part is different, and has its' own abilities, roles and function.

The unity comes from having one purpose in Christ.

This is not to say that we should accept anything that is contrary to God's Word, misuses it, or distorts its meaning into something false.

Our standard remains the same, for God's Word cannot be altered to accommodate the whims of culture.

But we have in Christ a safeguard against being easily offended. The love of Christ shields our hearts from harboring an easily offended spirit. His love covers a multitude of offenses.

An offended spirit is unhealthy for our emotional state; this is why forgiveness is essential for our "well-being".

When we pray for those who have wronged us, His love grows in us. We grow stronger, and closer to Christ, and receive His blessing.

We see His perspective---and it is always good, because He is good.

"…with you Lord is unfailing love" Psalm 62:12

HIS YOKE

Farmers in third world countries may be more familiar with the imagery of a yoke, and what it means, but we have all probably seen pictures of oxen yoked together, or have seen it in movies. And in sugar cane country, we know about the dedication to harvest.

Jesus is still looking for laborers in His harvest field, which is the world. He says, "Take my yoke upon you and learn from me, for I am gentle and humble in heart, and you will find rest for your souls." Matthew 11:29

A yoke binds two oxen together for service, and it keeps them going in the same direction.

Some people are afraid to surrender their lives to Christ because they fear his yoke; they think of Him as harsh, hard, abusive, and overbearing.

He is not harsh; He does not load us down, or abuse His servants. He cares about us, and gives us rest. He is gentle and humble, and His yoke is not unpleasant. Matthew 11:30

We are yoked to His incredible strength, and if we stumble or fall down, He is right there to pick us up. We are working *with* Him, not just for Him----it is His yoke.

His work gives us a purpose in our lives greater than ourselves. It is an honor and a privilege that we are chosen and invited to be part of His work.

And He gives us the power to be and do all that He asks, through the gift of the Holy Spirit, when we surrender our lives to Him.

The "yoke" of the world is a huge burden; it brings sorrow and pain that crushes us under its weight. This is because we are valued only for temporary usefulness, and not for ourselves.

Jesus loves us for ourselves; He welcomes and appreciates our uniqueness, because He designed us. He knows we have a need to be useful, but He does not love us only for our usefulness.

It is impossible to live up to the expectations of people, but the Lord gives us His grace to enable us to live up to His expectations. And then He rewards us for doing so!

When we are yoked with Jesus, we are safe from ourselves. The most dangerous thing to us is our own unbridled desire! I John 2:15-17

Some man-made religions of the world teach that you must get rid of all your desires in order to be righteous. This is impossible because the desire to be righteous is a desire!

The only thing that saves us is surrender of ourselves to the only One who can change our desires.

He gives us Himself----His love and friendship----when we surrender to Him.

"Whom have I in heaven but you? I desire you more than anything on earth. My health may fail, and my spirit may grow weak, but God remains the strength of my heart; he is mine forever." Psalm 73:25-26 NLT

PRIDE AND PREJUDICE

I'm a Jane Austen fan. Yes, I know her books depict the "social mores" of her time---but they also show the folly of human nature through her characters. Her story exposes how we make assumptions based on false perceptions and it becomes prejudice.

We do it with some things or people in the Bible, too! We've heard a certain explanation concerning a Bible verse or person, and ever after we view them through those "glasses."

If we're too proud to learn something new, we won't grow. We have to keep exploring God's Word for its hidden treasures. For example, look at Naomi in the book of Ruth.

I have often heard her spoken of in very negative terms; I have heard it said that she represents the backslider. We endured some criticism for naming our daughter Naomi because of this attitude.

I want to see God's Word for what it is---and not through the glasses of predetermined prejudice. After studying the book of Ruth carefully, I see Naomi differently than what is typically thought of her.

We are led by some to believe that Naomi was a failure, and that Ruth was the heroine. Who influenced whom? Whose faith and courage was it that influenced Ruth to leave her homeland and go to a foreign country? Who taught this Moabite girl to love the Lord if it was not Naomi?

It was not a sin when Naomi followed her husband to Moab because of the famine. It was not punishment from God when her loved ones died. The Lord blessed her with a daughter-in-law like Ruth, who had come to love Naomi very much---and to love Naomi's God. If Naomi had a weak character, I don't think she would have evoked such a response in this young woman.

Naomi tested both Ruth and Orpah when it was time to go back to Israel. Ruth's faith proved genuine and she went with Naomi into an unknown land where she might be ostracized. I believe that Naomi's faith in the Lord must have been Ruth's example. Despite the sorrow that Naomi had gone through, she still trusted in the Lord and returned home to Israel.

Once they were in Israel, Ruth was willing to follow the advice of her mother-in-law; again, I believe it was because she recognized the Lord's presence and guidance was with Naomi. Ruth trusted Naomi's decisions and Naomi's love for her. There had to be a reason for such trust.

The Lord rewarded Naomi's faith with a grandson who became the ancestor of King David, and a part of the lineage of the Messiah.

Her story of courage and hope after tragedy still inspires me, and makes me realize that it is not just Ruth who can be a role model for people that we teach.

And it is also a reminder to look beyond the prejudice towards people, and see them as the treasure God made them to be.

TODAY

God is our God TODAY.

He is not a "someday" God.

His help and comfort is available TODAY.

"God is our refuge and strength, an ever-present help in trouble." Ps 46:1

He IS, and He is PRESENT.

"Very truly I tell you," Jesus answered, "before Abraham was born, I am!" John 8:58

Jesus told the thief on the cross who believed in Him: "today you will be with me in paradise." Luke 23:43

Jesus told Zacchaeus: "Today salvation has come to this house..." Luke 19:9

Jesus taught us to pray: "Give us today our daily bread." Matthew 6:11

And He warns us: "Today, if you hear his voice, do not harden your hearts...." Hebrews 3:15

He commands us: "But encourage one another daily, as long as it is called "Today,".... Hebrews 3:13

Battle in prayer for the victories you long for, TODAY.

THE HORROR OF THAT MOMENT

I say moment, but it might have felt more like an eternity.

That moment in time WAS the crux of eternity.

For a moment, our fate hung in the balance. Jesus was in the Garden of Gethsemane, and He was in anguish. His sweat became drops of blood in his desperation.

It wasn't just the horrendous physical pain of crucifixion that He dreaded, though He had a human body like ours.

It wasn't just the shame of looking like a failure and the ridicule that would be heaped upon Him.

It wasn't just the disgrace of appearing naked before public view, and dying as a criminal. It was more than that, if a worse suffering could even be conceived.

His dread was the horror of that moment when He would be separated from His Father in Heaven.

It was His Father's love and approval that had been His strength during his entire sojourn as a human on the earth.

The reason for the impending separation was even more devastating.

For that moment in time, He would become the sin that any human has ever committed or will commit. It was as if He would inhale everything that brought evil and death to this planet. He would become every lie and deception, every act of cruelty and selfishness, every murder and every rotten, perverted, unjust, unkind thing that we say or do.

For the Son of God who is absolute pure Love and Goodness, this was the worst nightmare of all.

And then---to see His Father turn away from Him in that moment because of the revolting thing He had become----He could hardly bear the thought of enduring this horror, this excruciating torment that awaited Him.

But He did it.......for me.....and for you.

Make up your mind that you won't cause Him more pain----- instead, give Him your life.

He paid this price to set us free from the bondage of sin.

He paid this price to give us a new life with Him.

You are His joy.

"…let us run with perseverance the race marked out for us, fixing our eyes on Jesus, the pioneer and perfecter of faith. For the joy set before him he endured the cross, scorning its shame, and sat down at the right hand of the throne of God." Hebrews 12:1-2

GRATEFUL

Thank you Lord that our hearts are safe with You.

You have proved Your love to us.

You have given Your life to us.

You have chosen us to be with You forever.

You have esteemed us and honored us with Your love.

You have blessed us with your benefits and grace in an immeasurable way.

How could we ever neglect to appreciate such a love as this?

And what You ask in return is that we would love deeply our brothers and sisters in Christ.

May we not fail You in this, but increase in this expression of gratitude.

Give us more of Your Spirit to combat our innate selfish nature.

Continually set our hearts free by the power of Your Spirit and Your truth.

You give us the treasure of intimacy with Yourself, and this shows how much You value us.

I pray we would appreciate You far more----and realize what it cost You to give us this.

DESIRES

A friend recently expressed in words the same longing of my heart: The desire to see and know Jesus more....

Not as my "idea" of Him, or as I have imagined Him to be;

Not as others have portrayed as their idea of Him; but to see and know Him as He really is. He is who He says He is.

The revelation of who He is has been given to us in His Word, and He has given us a Teacher and Revealer: the Holy Spirit.

We want to feel that burning in our hearts at the words of Jesus, like the disciples on the road to Emmaus felt when Jesus spoke.

They didn't know who He was at first, but then their "eyes" were opened. They knew Him then.

They didn't understand His purposes until then, or His mission. It was another one of His "surprises" when He showed up!

He took time to be with these confused discouraged disciples, who didn't know what to believe anymore. (Luke 24)

If we take time to be with Him, I think He will show up! He said He would.

"For where two or three gather in my name, there am I with them." Matthew 18:20

There is nothing like hearing His voice.

ENDURANCE

We all like to buy things that will last---products that won't break right away. Usually the company that makes the item puts it through some extremely rough tests of endurance.

David was God's chosen one for a high calling, but first he had to go through many tough tests of endurance. He had to endure many years of scorn and disgrace.

In the 69th Psalm, David writes about this experience in verses 19-20. In the 21st verse, it becomes a prophecy, and the affliction of the Messiah is revealed.

It seems that scorn and disgrace are part of the preparation for a calling from God. To many in his nation, David was considered a scoundrel, a disloyal traitor, and a rebel. Few, I think, knew the real reason for David's expulsion from the king's palace, and must have assumed the worst about him.

David could not defend himself in this respect, and so he was viewed as an outlaw. David spent years being misrepresented and of no esteem to those in positions of authority, the elite, and the nobility. Though he had done no wrong, he was disliked and distrusted by those he had formerly served. He was out of their favor.

But he always had the favor of God.

Dishonor is something we may have to suffer as a servant of God. The Lord went through this, too, and He does not rely on the opinions of man. He is with us during those times; He is our comfort, our confidence, and our confidante, since He himself has suffered this.

"Know that the LORD has set apart his faithful servant for himself" Psalm 4:3. Sometimes it is a time of isolation that will become a transformation-----like the cocoon of a butterfly. When He changes you, it is undeniable and irrefutable.

Perhaps there was more in you than you realized, and He draws it out through suffering.

Of course, there will be a reckoning for those who do not recognize His presence, but He is merciful towards our blunders. And we must be merciful to one another.

Like a master craftsman or artist, He will not leave us alone until He is satisfied with our completion. And that will not be until the end of our earthly existence!

Christ endured the Cross, despising its' shame. Hebrews 12:2. And He had certainly done no wrong! I think this means He disregarded the shame, because He knew the greatness of God's plan. He was willing to put up with the shame, in order to fulfill the Father's plan.

And so, part of our training may involve enduring false accusation, a decline of reputation, and other sorts of injustices. I think that it would be better to go through this ignominy, than to live in a painless state that is ignorant and blind to His purposes. We are in His hands, to shape or mold as He pleases.

"in quietness and trust is your strength". Isaiah 30:15

THE SEAL OF APPROVAL

In the past, kings validated the authority of a document with their official seal—a definitive mark pressed into hot wax.

In modern culture, legal documents are still authorized by the stamp of a notary's seal. High quality products are distinguished by a particular trademark, which ensures the value of the product, and attests to the approval of its maker.

A seal still stands for authenticity, value, and ownership.

If you belong to Christ---and that entails obediently serving Him--- you have HIS SEAL OF APPROVAL.

This might sound like an audacious statement to some, but it is not based on our own merit. This Seal of Approval is based on the qualities of Someone far superior, who deigns to live in us.

It is the presence of his Holy Spirit that allows us to pass the inspection of the most scrutinous of all----our Maker.

You are under His authority. He claims you as His own. You have extreme value. His Word is your legacy.

"And you also were included in Christ when you heard the message of truth, the gospel of your salvation. When you believed, you were marked in him with a seal, the promised Holy Spirit, who is a deposit guaranteeing our inheritance until the redemption of those who are God's possession---to the praise of his glory." Ephesians 1:13-14

"Now it is God who makes both us and you stand firm in Christ. He anointed us, set his seal of ownership on us, and put his Spirit in our hearts as a deposit, guaranteeing what is to come." 2 Corinthians 1:21-22

ORIGINAL YOU

There is only one example of You, and that is You!

You're the only You---so don't try to be a copy of someone else. A copy of a masterpiece is never as valuable as an original. You are His original masterpiece!

Ask the Lord to help you be the best portrayal of You!

"Take delight in the Lord, and he will give you the desires of your heart." Psalm 37:4

That means He will give you HIS glorious desires! We cannot delight ourselves in the Lord to get our own desires fulfilled, because delight in Him and selfish desires don't mix. They are contrary to each other.

When you delight yourself in the Lord, your heart will change and His desires become yours. We are created in His image, so the best example of You, the most authentic example of original You, is a reflection of Him.

If we are hard and dry, or cold and critical, we are not yet the person that people are meant to see. Let us allow the Lord to soften us with His love, warm us with His peace, and shape us with His joy, so that all can clearly see His handiwork.

THE RACE OF GRACE

Negative opinions are like heavy chains on our spirits....it's hard to run a race with those hanging on you.

And we are in a race to the finish line....it's the Race of Grace, and the Finish Line is God's destiny and future for us in Heaven.

We are meant to aid each other along in this race, not to weigh each other down. Ecclesiastes 4:10

Anyone who holds another back to make sure that he gets ahead is going against God's principles for this race.

If we make someone stumble or fall because of a negative opinion, it is illegal in this race. 1 John 2:10

We are not competing against other believers in this race; we are competing against the enemy of our souls, and his schemes.

Negative opinions of each other only aid the enemy, because a negative attitude towards people drains their energy and depletes their strength. It does not increase effectiveness.

Negative attitudes cause a downward spiral---potential is destroyed and fruit is lost. Nothing good is gained by it; so why practice this? It is not God's wisdom.

Ten out of the twelve spies Joshua sent in to Canaan, came back with a negative report and prevented the people of God from realizing their potential!

God is a very positive Person! "For no matter how many promises God has made, they are "Yes" in Christ. And so through him the "Amen" is spoken by us to the glory of God." 2 Corinthians 1:20

"Therefore, since we are surrounded by such a great cloud of witnesses, let us throw off everything that hinders and the sin that so easily entangles. And let us run with perseverance the race marked out for us, fixing our eyes on Jesus, the pioneer and perfecter of faith. For the joy set before him he endured the cross, scorning its shame, and sat down at the right hand of the throne of God." Hebrews 12:1-2

"For the joy set before him, he endured the cross...."

It was Joy from Heaven that kept Him going to the end, and that's a very positive thing.

There will be negative circumstances; there is no denying that. And our training---our discipline for this race---may be unpleasant at times and seem contrary to His promises.

But Jesus has a continual positive attraction to us! He is pulling us to Him with His joy. His love for those who believe in Him is the most positive thing in this world.

Hold on to Heaven's joy!

On your mark....get set....Go!!

LEFT-OVERS

Abraham and his nephew Lot were on a journey together to the land of Canaan. When their flocks and herds became too great to share the same pasture land, they had to separate and go different ways.

Abraham gave his nephew first choice, and Lot chose what looked like the best, most fertile land----and Abraham took what was left-over.

Today we look at Lot's choice and immediately think of his choice as very selfish. Do you think Lot thought so? Maybe not---maybe his rationale went something like this: "I'm the next generation, the up-and-coming leader, and this is the most promising area. It will be my responsibility to provide for our families, and I need to make a wise choice for the good of all. Abraham is aging, and may not be able to handle all that will be produced in the future from this fertile land." So Lot gave Abraham the left-overs.

And Abraham probably smiled to himself; he had been friends with the Lord for a long time now. He knew what God can do with the left-overs, the discards, the seemingly useless.

Let's look at the relationship between Abraham and Lot. Abraham took his nephew with him, when the Lord told Abraham to leave his idolatrous home country and seek a relationship with Him in a new country. Evidently, Abraham had a nurturing relationship with Lot; he took him along and trained him in the business of raising livestock.

By the time they separated, Lot was successful and had his own flocks and herds. Had he forgotten who had trained him and taught him and given him resources to start with? It seems he thought of Abraham as unnecessary for his life now---maybe outdated. Lot was moving closer to the city---he would have the advantage of more progressive ideas.

Lot was caught up in his own role of leadership of his personnel who managed the flocks. Perhaps he thrived on his own sense of importance, and thought he didn't need Abraham anymore.

But he was wrong. And when Lot was in serious trouble from an enemy attack, it was Abraham and his servants who went after the enemy, defeated them, and rescued Lot.

It was Abraham who interceded for Lot during another disaster, and the Lord sent His angels to save Lot and his family from destruction.

Styles of clothing, furniture, houses, and music all change; but the anointing from the Spirit of God does not ever go out of style. God's power is never out-of-date or irrelevant.

The gifts of the Holy Spirit are never out dated, or unnecessary. Do not "retire" spiritually as you get older! The next generation needs this anointing, and they need to see it in operation. They need to see that "fight" in you against the enemy to rescue souls caught in the enemy's trap! They need to see your wisdom and strategy from the Holy Spirit to win battles. They need to hear you intercede.

Older generation, you are not left-overs; you are the foundation.

The story of Abraham is found in Genesis chapters 11-25.

I'M POSITIVE

Are you sure? "Definitely maybe" is what the world replies to this, and so we have relative morality, and situational ethics, and conditional "love" in the culture of the world.

Faith is always positive and never negative. There is no way we can believe the promises of God and remain negative! Faith trusts in God's character, and that He will do what He says.

It is the enemy who tries to negate God's Word with cynicism---something he has done from the beginning of the world.

Oh, that we would trust in the Lord's goodness like little children do!....that our hearts would not become cynical and negative due to the evil around us.

God is the God of Hope; and hope is not negative. It does not disappoint us, or it would cease to be hope. Hope encourages.

"And hope does not put us to shame, because God's love has been poured out into our hearts through the Holy Spirit, who has been given to us." Romans 5:5

"May the God of hope fill you with all joy and peace as you trust in him, so that you may overflow with hope by the power of the Holy Spirit." Romans 15:13

"Why, my soul, are you downcast? Why so disturbed within me? Put your hope in God, for I will yet praise him, my Savior and my God." Psalm 42:5

When we sing to the Lord, we are showing our faith in His goodness! It is a positive demonstration of our hope in Him.

So I will sing to Him with all of my being; with all of my heart.

"I will sing of the Lord's great love forever; with my mouth I will make your faithfulness known through all generations." Psalm 89:1

"I will sing to the LORD all my life; I will sing praise to my God as long as I live." Psalm 104:33

"Sing to him, sing praise to him; tell of all his wonderful acts." Psalm 105:2

The psalmist says he is sure of two things:

"One thing God has spoken, two things I have heard: "Power belongs to you, God, and with you, Lord, is unfailing love"" Psalm 62:11-12

God is for us, not against us----He is always positive.

LET THE GLASS GO....

In 1844, Hans Christian Anderson published his fairy tale known as "The Snow Queen." It was a tale of good versus evil, and a story depicting how the love of a friend conquered evil and rescued the captive friend from evil's terrible effects.

In the original story, an evil troll has an enchanted mirror. It represents the ugly, evil way he looks upon the world. One day, he drops the mirror and it breaks....and the shards of glass fall down everywhere upon the world.

In whosoever eye the shards of glass lodge, that person immediately begins to see the world in the evil way the troll does. The affected person sees other people as evil and worthless.

It's just a fairy tale, but it reminds me of some things.

The enemy wants us to see ourselves through his enchanted mirror.

He wants us to look into this tainted mirror and see ourselves as a "nobody".

He does not want us to know how deeply and intensely the Lord loves us.

This enemy does not want us to know that the Lord desires to call us His own, and that He offers us His intimate love....

The shards of glass in our eyes cause us to view others in the same way.

We see them as unworthy, as undesirable, as despicable…when they are the objects of God's love. We see them as the enemy wants us to see them.

With this shard embedded in our eyes, we see others through anger, resentment, jealousy, contempt, and callousness. We project onto them an evil image, which keeps us from seeing them as they really are.

Jesus talked about our sight---and about the person who tried to remove a splinter from someone's eye---but the person couldn't see well enough to do that, because he has a beam of wood stuck in his own eye. Matthew 7:4

In the fairy tale, once the shard of glass was removed from the person's eye, that person could see again with eyes of love and compassion for other people. Pain and hurt was gone.

When we see people through the eyes of Jesus, and not like the world's looking glass, we will be able to respect each person and their relationship with the Lord…or His desire to have a relationship with them.

The way we "see" affects everything.

"The eye is the lamp of the body. If your eyes are healthy, your whole body will be full of light." Matthew 6:22

REMEMBER ME...

One day as I was worshiping, I felt the Lord say this to me: "You have My heart." I was amazed and in awe of Him. How could He think so much about me?

I know that He meant that I have His love and affection; I also think that He meant I have His heart of passion and His desires. (That is only possible because He lives in me.)

I can think of nothing better to have; I can think of nothing better than to think like Jesus, feel like Jesus, and speak like Jesus.

I could never think or feel like He does, except for the power of the Holy Spirit. Oh, come and fill us! Oh, to think more like a citizen of Heaven.

The Lord is not exclusive; this is not for some special elite group. This is for everyone who wants to know Him.

I thought of the thief on the cross next to Jesus who realized who Jesus is, and he said: "Lord, remember me when You come into Your kingdom." Luke 23:42-43 NKJV

And Jesus responded: "Today you will be with me...."

He is so personal.

He is thinking about you today.....and every day.

"How precious are your thoughts about me, O God. They cannot be numbered! I can't even count them; they outnumber the grains of sand! And when I wake up, you are still with me!" Psalm 139:17-18 NLT

THE CHILD GREW

Luke 2:40 tells us that the child grew.

The baby in the manger became......a child.

This was not an insignificant time in His human existence. The way that Jesus treated children when He became an adult has had a great impact on our American culture.

This is not so in other cultures; children are abused and used in horribly degrading ways without any remorse from their violators. The people who perpetrate these despicable acts have been trained to think of children as devoid of value because children are defenseless. These cultures value aggression, and those who are powerless are considered worthless.

Jesus grew.

He was completely human, and completely God-----not half in half. He grew in body and spirit---He became strong and healthy in both ways, and increased in wisdom and in favor with God and man. (Luke 2:52)

The way that He grew in wisdom is the same way that we will grow in our spirits. We grow through revelation; as Jesus reveals Himself to us through His Word.

"The secret [of the sweet, satisfying companionship] of the Lord have they who fear (revere and worship) Him, and He will show them His covenant *and* reveal to them its [deep, inner] meaning." Psalm 25:14 AMPC

The world can read His parables, but He reveals the meaning to His disciples---the ones who have faith in Him.

"When he was alone, the Twelve and the others around him asked him about the parables. He told them, "The secret of the kingdom of God has been given to you. But to those on the outside everything is said in parables" Mark 4:10-11

"With many similar parables Jesus spoke the word to them, as much as they could understand. He did not say anything to them without using a parable. But when he was alone with his own disciples, he explained everything." Mark 4:33-34

Faith is much more than simply believing that God exists and that He is powerful. Faith believes in the character of God--- in His loving nature----in His goodness.

Faith believes that He is a rewarder. (Hebrews 11:6)

Abraham had this kind of relationship with God, and he is called the father of our faith. He believed in God's character.

Jesus demonstrated a Father/son relationship with God while He was here on earth; it was a true love relationship with the Creator of true love.

Though Jesus experienced discipline, it was a relationship of complete and total trust in the loving character of the Heavenly Father. And so should ours grow into this.

The better we know the Lord, the more we will see that He does not give conditional love based on our performance. He does not withhold love to punish and subdue us until there is compliance. And we should not discipline our children in this way either; we should nurture and train them in the same way that the Lord does for us.

IT'S A SECRET

"She's just a nobody," I heard the young man say about the aspiring artist. You may feel like a nobody, too.

All the world is running after satisfaction in recognition, fame, wealth, pleasure, and many other pursuits.....to be somebody.

But Christian believer, you have been given a Kingdom.

Think of That!

Only right now it is invisible; it is within you. Luke 17:20-21

It's a secret.....but you really are a Prince or a Princess.

Hold on----revelation is coming. The sons and daughters of the King---His heirs---will be revealed. Romans 8:19

"Do not be afraid, little flock, for your Father has been pleased to give you the kingdom." Luke 12:32

"And I confer on you a kingdom, just as my Father conferred one on me," Luke 22:29

"Listen, my dear brothers and sisters: Has not God chosen those who are poor in the eyes of the world to be rich in faith and to inherit the kingdom he promised those who love him?" James 2:5

The world may not think highly of you, but there is One who does. He chose you to inherit His kingdom.

Can you believe it?!

THE PERFECT MAN

"Son though he was, he learned obedience from what he suffered and once made perfect, he became the source of eternal salvation for all who obey him" Hebrews 5:8-9

The Son of God had to go through the "school of obedience" in his training as a human, in order to be the perfect high priest who himself has been tempted in every way that humans are tempted.

"For we do not have a high priest who is unable to empathize with our weaknesses, but we have one who has been tempted in every way, just as we are—yet he did not sin." Hebrews 4:15

He never gave in to the temptation, but He suffered by being tempted. "Because He himself suffered when he was tempted, he is able to help those who are being tempted." Hebrews 2:18 We see a picture of this in Matthew 4.

He had to experience all the complications and "hassles" of this human life. Hebrews 2:10

I think that Jesus had to experience the discipline of going to school as a child, the discipline of learning a skill and trade as a young man, and throughout, having to learn the art of living with a human family. This included obedience as a child, interacting with siblings, and caring for elderly parents.

Can you imagine the One who helped create the universe having to learn about math and physics? The One who designed gravity, time, space, and the theory of relativity had to submit to learning all the formulas and equations.

The One who invented water and created soil probably had to deal with getting dirty and obtaining enough water for their needs. The One who created trees had to learn the process of making wood into furniture. He had to deal with the practical issues of life from a human perspective.

In Matthew 4, we see that Satan tempted Jesus to skip all that and take the "easy way out." Jesus obeyed the Father always and refused to listen to the enemy's suggestions.

Jesus knew the Kingdoms of the world would be His---but only through the Father's way. He knew that taking risks to exploit God's power was not God's way. He showed that satisfying the desires of the body should never take precedence over our need for God's Word.

Jesus lived to be the perfect example of devotion to God. He defeated the enemy's temptations with the truth of God's Word. He showed that maturity is the result of being able to distinguish between good and evil. This takes practice to train ourselves to distinguish it. It takes preparation and study of God's Word.

"But solid food is for the mature, who by constant use have trained themselves to distinguish good from evil." Hebrews 5:14

School is not just about learning facts and subjects; it is more about learning discipline we will need for maturity. And Jesus Himself went through it in order to help us with the "hassles" of life.

He cares about us and for us.

RELIGION IS DEAD

The secular world says that Jesus started a new religion.

No; He came to show us that religion can't save us. The secular world also implies that God is irrelevant or dead. He's not; it is religion that is dead.

The religious leaders at the time that Jesus showed up, thought of Jesus as a rebel. He broke all their rules and did not respect their authority.

These Pharisees preferred their status in society, over truth. They liked their religious role because it gave them the means to control people. They wanted to keep people subjected to their system of religious slavery.

The Pharisees wanted Jesus to submit to their will; but He was submitted to God's will. So there was conflict. When the Pharisees saw they could not silence Jesus, they set out to destroy Him.

Jesus died at the hands of merciless men, to give us His mercy, and to deliver us from the weight of our sin.

Religion cannot relieve us of the burden of sin; it adds to the heavy burden we already carry. Religion is lifeless and does not refresh us; it makes us weary and discouraged.

Jesus says: "Come to me, all you who are weary and burdened, and I will give you rest. Take my yoke upon you and learn from me, for I am gentle and humble in heart, and you will find rest for your souls. For my yoke is easy and my burden is light." Matthew 11:28-30

Jesus conquered death and He is alive. He can give us life. Religion can't because it is lifeless.

Spiritual birth cannot be imparted by people; it comes from the Giver of Life: God.

Jesus said He is the way, the truth, and the LIFE. John 14:6

Knowing Jesus is life.....Real life.

"Now this is eternal life: that they know you, the only true God, and Jesus Christ, whom you have sent." John 17:3

I want to know Him better!

FAITH

It looked like the answer was "no". It sounded like an insult. It appeared to be rejection ---….and yet, it wasn't.

It was one of the strangest conversations recorded in the Bible, and I used to be very puzzled by it.

A Canaanite woman came to Jesus and asked Him to heal her daughter. He didn't even answer her. The disciples got tired of her pleading, and asked Jesus to make her go away.

Then He said, "I was sent only to the lost sheep of Israel." This did not deter the woman. She came and knelt before Him, and implored Him: "Lord, help me!" she said.

He said, "It is not right to take the children's bread and toss it to the dogs." "Yes it is, Lord," she said, "Even the dogs eat the crumbs that fall from their masters' table."

How could this extremely kind God-man, who went around doing good and healing all who were oppressed by the devil, say such a thing to this woman?

Then Jesus said, "Woman, you have great faith! Your request is granted."

Recently, I realized what Jesus was doing.

Jesus knows what is in our hearts; He knew what she would answer. He was creating a picture of faith for all of us.

This brings me to another realization and question: are our lives a picture of faith?

Would we cling to Jesus-----even when His disciples complain about us, think of us as only a bother, and wish we would just go away?

Will we still believe in His love for us when He doesn't answer us right away?

Will we persist in our prayer and worship because we believe in His goodness, even when He seems to be exclusive?

He will test our faith. Do not give up; don't stop believing in His character, and keep asking for the things that you know He wants to do, to deliver people from bondage.

This woman knew Jesus was Lord; and she knew also that He was capable of delivering her daughter, and also that it was His mission on earth to deliver people from satanic oppression. So she persisted, and she received from Jesus.

This is faith. Faith will not let go of Jesus; it will persist in prayer, and faith will call Him Lord even when we are treated as unworthy of His attention.

Faith has a positive response in the face of negativity, because faith believes in His goodness no matter what situations look like.

This story is from Matthew 15:21-28.

BELONGING

I enjoy watching all of the many expressions our granddaughter makes---it delights me to see her enjoy life and what she is experiencing.

I wonder if this is a glimpse into how our Heavenly Father looks at His children, once the curse of sin is reversed, and we have a relationship with Him.

When we are around people who only tolerate us and don't enjoy us, it can make us "lose sight" of the way the Lord feels about us. Jesus wants to repair the damage done, and make our hearts like a child's.

We belong to Him!

"Jesus said, "Let the little children come to me, and do not hinder them, for the kingdom of heaven belongs to such as these." Matthew 19:14

He reveals secrets to us!

"At that time Jesus, full of joy through the Holy Spirit, said, "I praise you, Father, Lord of heaven and earth, because you have hidden these things from the wise and learned, and revealed them to little children. Yes, Father, for this is what you were pleased to do." Luke 10:21

We have permission to enter!

"Truly I tell you, anyone who will not receive the kingdom of God like a little child will never enter it." Luke 18:17

We are welcomed.

"Whoever welcomes one of these little children in my name welcomes me; and whoever welcomes me does not welcome me but the one who sent me." Mark 9:37

See His Kingdom like a child!

There is a story about toys that come alive in a little boy's room. The main toy character felt insecure until he discovered the mark of ownership----the name of his owner was written on the bottom of the toy character's shoe. Then the toy realized he was loved.

When we come to Christ, He marks us with the seal of ownership and we belong to Him.

"And you also were included in Christ when you heard the message of truth, the gospel of your salvation. When you believed, you were marked in him with a seal, the promised Holy Spirit, who is a deposit guaranteeing our inheritance until the redemption of those who are God's possession—to the praise of his glory." Ephesians 1:13-14

"Now it is God who makes both us and you stand firm in Christ. He anointed us, set his seal of ownership on us, and put his Spirit in our hearts as a deposit, guaranteeing what is to come." 2 Corinthians 1:21-22

THE MERCY UMBRELLA

We are most like the Heavenly Father when we are kind and forgiving---not when we demean others in a critical way.

It is the Lord's gentleness towards us that makes us strong. "You have also given me the shield of your salvation, and Your right hand has held me up; Your gentleness and condescension have made me great." Psalm 18:35 AMPC I believe this means strong or great, in character.

This kind of condescension is not out of haughtiness; it is out of compassion and pity for our need. The Lord Jesus was highly displeased with the Pharisees for their haughty superior attitude, and the way they said or thought things like this: "I'm glad I am not like Those people. It's too bad they don't do all the correct spiritual things like I do."

The Pharisees didn't know or recognize the character of God at all. They were following in the footsteps of the enemy instead of the Lord's---and they were not even aware of it.

But if we enter into the Lord's "salvation covenant", it is like we come under His Mercy Umbrella. There is nothing we could do to be worthy to enter the covenant---but there are requirements to enter: you must surrender yourself completely and let Him take you through His rebirth transformation. You have to trust Him and take this "leap of faith" into the unknown.

Something so wonderful and unexpected happens! You discover that you can finally understand the meaning of the words of His covenant---its Heavenly interpretation. The Bible suddenly becomes a revelation of the Lord's mercy.

Under His mercy umbrella, the Lord reveals Himself as the perfect Teacher. He is not the kind of Person who says, "You messed up. I don't want you around anymore." He patiently teaches us His way. He instructs us and guides us.

"Good and upright is the Lord; therefore he instructs sinners in his ways. He guides the humble in what is right and teaches them his way. All the ways of the Lord are loving and faithful toward those who keep the demands of his covenant." Psalm 25:8-10

This is life under the mercy umbrella. We are taught and guided by the Lord Himself---that shows His great humility. He reveals things to us---wonderful things in His Word.

Prosperity doesn't always mean worldly wealth---it can mean the satisfaction of spiritual blessings. We can give our children that kind of priceless inheritance!

Under the mercy umbrella, we begin to recognize iniquity in ourselves. Iniquity is defined by the word unfair. The more we understand the Lord's covenant, the more we realize when we are being unfair.

When we don't freely forgive others from our heart, we are being unfair. Don't try to make other believers pay to get forgiveness from you. Don't try to make them earn it.

This is what the person in "The Parable of the Unmerciful Servant" did to someone else---he had been forgiven, but he went out and tried to make someone else pay to get *his* forgiveness. When Jesus said, "Give and it will be given to you", He was talking about mercy and forgiveness, not money. Luke 6:37-38 Matthew 18:21-35

Live under the Mercy Umbrella.

LOVELY

Lord Jesus, I love who You are.

I love everything about You.

I especially love that You are changing me.....to be like You.

What a wonder that is!

How could I ever be like You?

But all things are possible through Your grace....and the power of the Holy Spirit.

There is No one who could ever compare to You in the depth and intensity of Your love for us-----Your fallen creatures------who deserved nothing.

Nothing except extinction.

And still Your mercy reaches out, even to those who rebel against You, hate You, and want nothing to do with You or Your ways.

They think Your love will stifle them......when in fact, it will free them.

They think that You will make them miserable and confine them in a rigid, religious box.

But sin is the cage that has trapped us----with lust, addictions, hate, and pride.

We are not free without Your love.

Our spirits have been warped, misshapen, contorted, and deformed by sin------we are freaks of sinful nature.

And the enemy relishes how he torments our minds and deceives us-----into thinking that the worst possible state would be in devotion to an overbearing demanding God.

Lord Jesus, when I met you, You gave me Hope.

And every lie, You turned back onto the enemy from whom it came.

You delivered me from my deep depression, from my loneliness, from my despair.

Your mercy became my Song.

I will sing it forever.

I will sing to You with all my heart, for You are the most beautiful Person I could ever know----

And You love me..........and He loves you, too.

"For the Lord is good and his love endures forever; his faithfulness continues through all generations." Psalm 100:5

TRANSFORMATION

Our relationship with the Lord is one of revelation.

As we spend time with Him, He reveals intimate things---
secrets of His Kingdom that He only shares with people who
prize Him and His kingdom.

The world can read His parables, but He reveals the
meaning to His children. This is our heritage.

This is how we grow in the Kingdom of God; Jesus reveals
Himself to us through His Word.

The contrast between His goodness and the culture of the
world becomes more and more visible.

Layers of deception and errors in perception are removed
more and more. He changes the way we think and feel about
attitudes and actions.

In effect, He shows us right from wrong, which is impossible
to "see" with our sin-damaged mind. It has to be spiritually
revealed.

Slowly He transforms us from our ignorant state to be like
Him. Sometimes the process is painful---we may go through
hurt, rejection, sorrow, disappointment, or difficult
circumstances.

But He does not leave us or forsake us. Hebrews 13:5

It is in those times we learn how to seek God diligently and
persistently. You can trust in His work----He always finishes
what He begins. There will be a transformation.

DELIVERANCE FROM DIS

When our redemption is complete, and our bodies are made new---our brains will be healed, and I believe we will all be "prodigies", with extraordinary intellect and abilities!

Our brains will operate the way they would have, before the fall of mankind into sin. (Genesis 3)

We will be delivered from DIS. Every bad thing that I can think of begins with dis!

Disability	Discouragement	Disgrace	Disqualify
Dislike	Disagreeable	Disaster	Discredit
Disarray	Disappointing	Disbelief	Discarded
Disease	Disconnected	Discord	Discontent
Disdain	Disadvantage	Distrust	Disrespect
Dismay	Discrimination	Dishonor	Displeased
Disorder	Disapproval	Disrepair	Disparage
Distress	Disorganized	Disturbed	Dishonest
Distort	Dissatisfied	Disgust	Disinterest
Disown	Disillusion	Disinherit	Discomfort
Dismal	Disobedient	Disrupt	Disfigure

I'm sure there are more----but that's enough of Dis!

I am looking forward to no more of dis.

REFLECTION

Most of my posts come from thoughts I write in my journal in the morning. In that sense, they are reflections—musings; meditations on the Lord and His Word. But today I was thinking of the double meaning of the word: as believers we are meant to be a reflection of the Lord and His character.

He called us out of the world's culture into a Heavenly culture; we are citizens of the Heavenly Kingdom. Yet because we are born and raised in the world's culture, it seems to take a long time to stop thinking like the old system and think like the culture of Heaven.

The early disciples were like that, too. One day they were pointing out to Jesus all the magnificence of the Temple, thinking He would be impressed. He wasn't.

He told them, "not one stone here will be left on another;" Their reaction was panic. "When, Lord?" they implored of Him. But He wouldn't tell them. (Matthew 24:1-44)

Another time, He sat by the offering area and watched as people put their gifts into the offering treasury. He pointed out one poor woman to the disciples. She had put in 2 small copper coins, worth less than a penny. "This poor widow has put more into the treasury than all the others," Jesus commented to the disciples, even though there were many who had given large sums of money. (Mark 12:41-43)

What impresses the world is not what impresses the Lord. Sometimes we get distracted by the values of the world, and we instinctively try to impress the world with "success".

Just when we think we have this Kingdom thing all figured out, Jesus in effect tells us, "Get out of that box. I'm bigger than that". We can never figure Him out----but we don't have to. All we have to do is follow Him.

Our greatest goal and best aspiration is to be a true reflection of Him---not just individually, but as a group as well. Just as Jesus obeyed His Heavenly Father to accurately portray Him, our obedience to the Lord provides a reflection of Jesus.

God fulfilled Abraham's dream of having a son---an heir. Then one day the Lord told Abraham to kill his dream. Abraham was prepared to obey fully because he trusted in the character of God. God stopped him, but Abraham's willing obedience provided a picture—a reflection—of the character of God.

One day God would lay His own Son down on a wooden cross and nail Him to it by His own will----to become our sacrifice for sin. He saved us through His righteousness—His goodness.

I cannot figure out how a God who could make this entire universe would do that for such a tiny world full of tiny humans, who are so corrupted by an unrighteous nature.

As incredible as the Gospel sounds, I believe it.

And I believe that the privilege of having a love relationship with Jesus the Son of God is the greatest thing that could ever happen to a person.

This is an Eternal Gift.

A PRAYER FOR REFLECTION

Lord, drive out everything in us that would misrepresent You.

Remove anything that distorts Your image, and cripples the minds of Your children.

Replenish from Your Holy Spirit's storehouse every deficiency in our spirits that would stunt our growth.

Send the waves of Your glory to wash us, and the fires of Your heart to purify us.

Destroy any legalism that binds us to cruelty, and release Your peace to protect us from irritation with one another.

Stimulate us to acts of kindness and encouragement, prompted by Your love and goodness.

Let each person, like a piece of the puzzle, find their unique placement in this heavenly designed picture of Your face, so we can present You to the world around us. They need to see the real You.

"May God be gracious to us and bless us and make his face shine on us---so that your ways may be known on earth, your salvation among all nations." Psalm 67:1-2

YOUR HOUSE

When I was a teenager, I had an unhappy home.

I was despised.

I was rejected.

I was ridiculed.

I was sad and it was painful.

I was lonely.

I lived with people I could not trust.

Relief came from an unexpected source; it came from the One I had heard about most of my life, and mostly disregarded as irrelevant to my life. I was not looking for Him, but He looked for me.

I was ignorant of His love for me and His sacrifice for me, and this hurt Him, but He came to me. And when I met Him----really met Him----I found the One who understood me.

He was despised;

He was rejected;

He was ridiculed;

He was a man of sorrows and acquainted with grief. (Isaiah 53)

He had few real friends, and many of His peers did not respect Him. (John 6:66)

There were few people that He could really trust. (John 2:23-25)

When I went to a church where He was known, I found acceptance, love, appreciation, respect, joy, and a new family that I could trust. Church became Home. I can really relate to these verses:

"I am like an olive tree flourishing in the house of God; I trust in God's unfailing love for ever and ever." Psalm 52:8

"Lord, I love the house where you live, the place where your glory dwells." Psalm 26:8

It's not the building that is so special or sacred; it's His presence.

When the woman with the alabaster box broke it open and poured all the expensive perfume on Jesus, I'm sure she already knew that she would be ridiculed and criticized and possibly condemned for her actions.

Her love for Jesus and her gratitude to Him was greater than her fear of scorn or criticism or rejection. So she gave her best to Him.

That is what I want to do.

HONOR HIS BODY

Jesus was about to go through the grisly, intense, horrific torture of Roman crucifixion.

Yet He took time to eat with His friends. And He washed their feet! This was His example of endearment and gentleness. In that culture, washing someone's feet was a sign of hospitality and showed that you thought highly of your guest, although it was usually performed by a servant and not the Master of the house.

This is how God feels about us: He wants to wash our feet! He is gracious; He welcomes us and wants to give us His grace.

We need His grace. Ephesians 5:26 tells us that we need washing with the water of the Word, and Jesus is the Word of God. Peter wanted to decline having His Lord wash his feet, but Jesus insisted that Peter needed it. And we do, too.

Jesus expects us to welcome each other in the same way. He is our Lord, yet He offers us hospitality and intimate friendship---and expects us to do this for other people because He loves them dearly.

In the world, people go around trying to "fix" each other, because it makes them feel superior. So they specialize in finding flaws.

When they do, they capitalize on this flaw, and magnify every distinctive habit or personal quirk into the category of deficiency or disease! Labelling it as such gives them a sort of power. Now they can increase their own worth by discovering a "cure" for the "disease".

When they are truly promoted, the principles of the Kingdom of God eliminate the need of trying to "fix" each other to feel superior. Hostility is traded in for hospitality; harshness is traded in for gentleness, and derogatory labels are traded in for "terms of endearment."

People like to feel superior to others, especially if it makes them feel better about themselves. Yet even when people treat us badly, the Lord does not want us to start thinking we are better than they are.

We all have a common enemy who is out to make us stumble and fall. His plan is to make believers dislike one another. The enemy is an accuser---he goes around putting accusing and belittling thoughts about each other into the minds of believers.

Recognize his tactics and resist him in the power of the Spirit. The best way to defeat the enemy is to value each other, love one another and forgive offenses. Even erratic behavior can be a distress signal; so use discernment, not discrimination.

As believers, we are part of something---something bigger than ourselves----we are part of the Body of Christ.

Sometimes people develop a terrible habit of cutting themselves—they cut their bodies many times. When we cut other believers down, we are cutting the body of Christ.

We should take care of Christ's body with honor; we should become Body Guards who protect one another.

OVERCOME

Often, I have not realized that the negative emotions I was experiencing were happening because I was being oppressed by the enemy.

Have you ever felt like there was a "cloud"----a smothering heaviness over the church service?

Like you couldn't break through into God's presence?

I have. I felt like my lungs would not expand, and I could not sing out or worship freely. Yet I knew it could not be due to neglect of prayer or God's Word. I repented anyway.

I wondered if I had unknowingly offended the Lord. He quickly reminded me that He is not that fickle! He does not change His kindness and love towards me overnight.

Then I knew it was the enemy. The enemy comes to steal our joy! He tries to keep us from experiencing God's presence, for this is the joy which strengthens us.

"...for the joy of the Lord is your strength." Nehemiah 8:10

The enemy of our souls---and of our families---and of our church---and of our nation---wants to divert us into depression, and lull us into lethargy.

It's like the poppy fields in the Wizard of Oz----don't go to sleep!! You are the enemy's prey. Listen....to the Holy Spirit. He will direct you into the way you should go----God's path.

We have to stay alert and pray.

Do not sink into despair. The enemy wants us to disbelieve in the power of prayer, and quit praying. The power of God that is in you to pray, is greater than the one at work in the world.

"Little children (believers, dear ones), you are of God *and* you belong to Him and have [already] overcome them [the agents of the antichrist]; because He who is in you is greater than he (Satan) who is in the world [of sinful mankind]."
1 John 4:4 AMP

"You, dear children, are from God and have overcome them, because the one who is in you is greater than the one who is in the world." 1 John 4:4 (NIV)

God is greater than all the enemy's plots against us.

THE TRUTH

The enemy confuses us into believing that:

Insecurity = humility   Positive attitude = arrogance
Confidence = pride   Timidity = the fear of the Lord

What does please the Lord? That we believe: In His character, in His love for us, and in His faithfulness.

"And without faith it is impossible to please God, because anyone who comes to him must believe that he exists and that he rewards those who earnestly seek him."
Hebrews 11:6

The enemy knows that if we are insecure, he can keep knocking us down and bullying us and we will not recognize it as him. We will absorb the blame and not fight back.

The enemy of our souls uses intimidation to "freeze the assets"----the gifts in us that the Lord has given to us to use for His Kingdom. This enemy tries to deprive us of our legal benefits as God's heirs, through his lies.

The Lord wants us to develop confidence in our relationship with Him. This confidence comes from trusting His character and depending on His Holy Spirit for strength.

"Lean on, trust in, *and* be confident in the Lord with all your heart *and* mind and do not rely on your own insight *or* understanding." Proverbs 3:5 AMPC

Trust = confident assurance and reliance.

He is never untrue to His Word; He will fulfill every promise.

THE PRIVILEGE OF PRAYER

A young man I know asked a sincere question about prayer: Should we simply ask for God's will instead of begging Him for something we think we need or want?

That really is a big question.

I have been thinking about it ever since he asked. Here is what I thought of:

Prayer isn't just about asking; it's about becoming.

Our God is the one who made the universe in all its mind-boggling immensity.

Of course He doesn't "need" our prayers in order to carry out His will---or any human help at all.

He didn't "need" David's slingshot to take out that giant.

But He desires us to participate with Him in His work upon the earth, and gives us this privilege through prayer.

He changes our mindset through His Word so we can understand His desires better.

The more we seek Him in prayer, (not just answers) the more our faith grows, and as we trust him more, we get to participate more with Him.

As we get to know Him, His desires become ours, and we will have greater discernment about prayer.

"You who answer prayer, to you all people will come."
Psalm 65:2

NEW EVERY DAY

The Lord's compassion never fails; His mercies are NEW every morning!

"Because of the Lord's great love we are not consumed, for his compassions never fail. They are new every morning; great is your faithfulness." Lamentations 3:22-23

Every morning, I can wake up and know that He is there.
Every morning, I can count on His love.
Every morning, I can depend on His wisdom.

New things can be refreshing; like having some new clothes to replace the faded ones, or new furniture to replace the worn out ones, or a new car that runs better than the old one.

We like variety, too, so the Lord gives us the changing seasons in our weather.

Some people treat relationships with the same attitude as they have for furniture; they discard people. The Lord does not do this to us; He does not dispose of us----He renews us.

He is the God who will make all things new.

"He who was seated on the throne said, "I am making everything new!" Then he said, "Write this down, for these words are trustworthy and true." Revelations 21:5

He renews our strength. Isaiah 40:31

He renews our minds. Romans 12:2

He renews our hearts. 2 Corinthians 4:16

He renews our knowledge of Him. Colossians 3:10

Nothing on earth will last----except for the Lord's love. Everything on earth will decay and end----but what is given to the Lord, He will make new. There is new life in Him.

"We were therefore buried with him through baptism into death in order that, just as Christ was raised from the dead through the glory of the Father, we too may live a new life." Romans 6:4

In Christ, we have a Living Hope.

When our bodies wear out, He will provide new ones.

We will have a new home, prepared for us.

There is a new ending to our life story, because now Jesus is in it. He has changed the final scene.

"Praise be to the God and Father of our Lord Jesus Christ! In his great mercy he has given us new birth into a living hope through the resurrection of Jesus Christ from the dead, and into an inheritance that can never perish, spoil, or fade. This inheritance is kept in heaven for you,"   I Peter 1:3-4

WAKING UP

"Arise [from the depression and prostration in which circumstances have kept you---rise to a new life]! Shine (be radiant with the glory of the Lord), for your light has come, and the glory of the Lord has risen upon you!" Isaiah 60:1 AMPC

Picture this----We are lying alone in a silent hopeless tomb with no way to escape. The enemy of our souls kissed us with his poisonous lies, and we succumbed to sin and died a spiritual death. Then he sealed us off from Love with a heart as hard as rock. We lie there in the darkness, separated from God---dead in our sins and unaware of the truth.

Then came the Resurrection, and the wind of the Spirit began to blow.....And the glorious Light of Christ begins to penetrate through every crack....

I picture us waking up from the sleep of death.... when we hear the voice of Jesus call to us to come out....we stumble out into His light and truth....

And He sets us free from the grave clothes that entangled us....And He sets His seal upon us...the seal of Eternal Life.

"Where, O death, is your victory? Where, O death, is your sting?" 1 Corinthians 15:55

For even though our mortal bodies will die, we will be alive in Jesus. Forever.

No one can steal His life from us; it is His gift to us....no one can separate us from this Love that overcame death for us.

There is no One greater or stronger or more powerful than the One who conquered death.

So Rise and Shine! We too are risen---raised with Him to a new life. Hallelujah!

"For what I received I passed on to you as of first importance: that Christ died for our sins according to the Scriptures, that he was buried, that he was raised on the third day according to the Scriptures, and that he appeared to Cephas, and then to the Twelve." 1 Corinthians 15:3-5

"And you also were included in Christ when you heard the message of truth, the gospel of your salvation. When you believed, you were marked in him with a seal, the promised Holy Spirit" Ephesians 1:13

"And if the Spirit of him who raised Jesus from the dead is living in you, he who raised Christ from the dead will also give life to your mortal bodies because of his Spirit who lives in you." Romans 8:11

"We were therefore buried with him through baptism into death in order that, just as Christ was raised from the dead through the glory of the Father, we too may live a new life." Romans 6:4

"For the wages of sin is death, but the gift of God is eternal life in Christ Jesus our Lord." Romans 6:23

"The last enemy to be destroyed is death." 1 Corinthians 15:26

"The sting of death is sin, and the power of sin is the law. But thanks be to God! He gives us the victory through our Lord Jesus Christ." 1 Corinthians 15:56-57

LOSERS

The minute we stop believing God's Word, we become losers. Adam and Eve lost Paradise when they stopped believing what God said and became convinced He had misled them.

The same thing happens to us when we stop believing what God says….when what the secular community says sounds more plausible and sensible and rational to us than what God says; when the "justice" that the world promotes sounds more righteous.

We become losers.

"For whoever has, to him more shall be given; and whoever does not have, even what he has shall be taken away from him." Mark 4:25 NASB

This sounds like some kind of riddle. The answer is found, I believe, when you match it up to other things that Jesus tells us.

"Therefore everyone who hears these words of mine and puts them into practice is like a wise man who built his house on the rock. The rain came down, the streams rose, and the winds blew and beat against that house; yet it did not fall, because it had its foundation on the rock. But everyone who hears these words of mine and does not put them into practice is like a foolish man who built his house on sand. The rain came down, the streams rose, and the winds blew and beat against that house, and it fell with a great crash." Matthew 7:24-27

The wise person not only heard God's Word, but put it into practice.

We lose what we do not use.

The foolish person heard God's Word, but never applied it to his life. God's Word was not part of his decision-making, his motivations, or choices. He had nothing solid to build on; he had only the opinions of the society around him to influence and guide him. And his house—the refuge, the place of safety—fell apart.

Young people may be in environments where they hear a lot of God's Word, but once they leave that environment, they may lose what they heard if they do not put God's Word into practice. How can we help them realize this?

I don't want to see any more young people become losers. I know you don't want that either. It is not a battle of wits; it is a supernatural battle against deceptive spirits unleashed in our world. But God Himself has given us strategic weapons for this battle.

"We use God's mighty weapons, not worldly weapons, to knock down the strongholds of human reasoning and to destroy false arguments." 2 Corinthians 10:4 NLT

This must mean praying in the power of the Holy Spirit. Lord, please give us more of Your Spirit to intercede for people, in agreement with what the Spirit says. Romans 8:26-27

I believe we should also earnestly seek the supernatural gifts of the Holy Spirit. (I Corinthians 12)

THE GAME OF LIFE

Sometimes in this Game of Life, you have to go back to go forward.

Maybe you pulled a card of directions with misleading information, and you find yourself on a detour into an area of toxic substance!

It's a poisonous wasteland, so go back to the place before the detour. Go back to the spot where you were standing in the wholesomeness of the Gospel truth, and the goodness of Christ's love for His Body.

Go back to the simplicity and purity of God's Word, before the contamination from toxins of suspicion, duplicity, mistrust, and hostility. They blur our spiritual vision.

The Lord is so trustworthy! "For the word of the Lord is right and true; he is faithful in all he does." Psalm 33:4 "But the eyes of the Lord are on those who fear him, on those whose hope is in his unfailing love," Psalm 33:18.

He will take us back to the place where we lost our way in a detour.

God's peace detoxes our minds, and reorders our perceptions. Like the turn of a kaleidoscope, mental distress and confusion is changed into a beautiful design by His grace and peace. We can approach this game of life and its tasks with a different viewpoint, with a vision of His beauty and glory.

Stress and anxiety are also toxic elements in our world. These make it difficult for our spirits to breathe. The Lord's presence creates a shield-of-favor around us like a bubble filled with Heaven's atmosphere so we can breathe. So sing and worship Him with all of your energy! You will find the breath of Heaven.

When people come under the stress and anxiety of competing in the world's marketplace, even in spiritual matters, they can lose sight of the things that the Holy Spirit produces.

They can lose the sense of the Heavenly atmosphere and its' joy, and breathe in the world's toxins. It is a detour into Vanity Fair, where the emphasis is on appearance, attraction, relevance, and popularity. Its fruit is phony.

In Vanity Fair, the people are weighted down with more and more regulations and stipulations and instigations in order to keep up with the latest how-to methods and motivations.

They begin to follow a religion instead of Jesus.

Go back to the place where you lost sight of the Real goal in the game of life….and then make your next move, led by the Holy Spirit.

Go back, to go forward.

MEASURE

"You are my portion, Lord; I have promised to obey your words." Psalm 119:57

"I say to myself, "The Lord is my portion; therefore I will wait for him."' Lamentations 3:24

There are many references to measures and measuring in the Bible. When the verse uses the word "portion" it can mean a measure or an amount, or it can mean an allotment, as in an inheritance.

But the Lord doesn't measure and dole out small doses of Himself. He is saying, "You can have all you want of Me!"

The Lord's love cannot be contained and measured; it is as infinite as the universe.

We can't measure Him to any other experiences in life; no one else can be compared to Him.

We can say like Oliver Twist, "Please, Sir, I want some more,"----and we will never be punished for this, or denied.

Sometimes we are just not hungry enough---we are too full of other things to want more of Him. Oh, Lord, empty us and enlarge our hearts to hold more of You.

"...And I pray that you, being rooted and established in love, may have power, together with all the Lord's holy people, to grasp how wide and long and high and deep is the love of Christ, and to know this love that surpasses knowledge--- that you may be filled to the measure of all the fullness of God." Ephesians 3:17-19

GOD IS GREAT, GOD IS GOOD

Remember this little poem prayer? The words are simple, yet profound.

Our nature is so different from the Lord's, that it is hard to comprehend how good He is.

Even our understanding of goodness is faulty because of our corrupted nature.

Unconditional love is an enormous concept for these finite human minds to grasp. There is the tendency to modify it, in order to put it within the realm of our human experience.

But it is definitely not of this world!

When the devil attacks our minds to undermine our faith, the first thing he tries is to make us believe that God is not really good---so that we won't trust or obey the Lord.

God's love is so holy and pure that He could never have an intimate relationship with the nasty creatures we became through the downfall of man. Sin looks like leprosy to God----something horrible and disgusting.

Only an extreme act of Holy Love could remove our filth and shame---so He sacrificed Himself, so that He could love us.

That is unconditional love.

"But God demonstrates his own love for us in this: While we were still sinners, Christ died for us." Romans 5:8

"We were God's enemies, but he made us his friends through the death of his Son." Romans 5:10 GNT

IN MY RIGHT MIND

I once read of a mother who told her young daughter that her shoes were on the wrong feet. The little girl looked very perturbed and replied, "But these are the only feet I have!"

I'm sure you have heard of the expression, "He's not in his right mind". I guess that means he is in his Wrong mind!

I think that is what our enemy, the devil, does to us: he tries to give us the wrong mind.

The Scriptures warn us that the way we think affects the way we act. "For as he thinks in his heart, so is he." Proverbs 23:7 NKJV

God's Word tells us that we can have the mind of Christ! 1 Corinthians 2:16

The enemy does not want us to experience that reality. He corrupts our minds with lies, depression and discouragement----his deadly mental viruses that cause malfunctions.

If that doesn't work, he tries to sneak in with his Trojan horses (deception) and his malicious malware that causes mistrust, suspicion, and fatal errors.

Resist him----that means fight back---so he can't steal from you and make you lose your right mind!

Being "in your right mind" means having true thinking. Truth comes from God's Word; Jesus is the way, the Truth, and the life. (John 14:6) Every attitude we have about life, ourselves and others must come from God's Word.

Every day, I need an "update" from God's Word---I need spiritual reprogramming by the Holy Spirit. He has the best malware elimination! His filter can find those corrupted mental files, quarantine them, then eliminate them.

I need the Holy Spirit to "scan" me to see if there is any spiritual virus in me, and clean me.

"Search me, God, and know my heart; test me and know my anxious thoughts. See if there is any offensive way in me, and lead me in the way everlasting." Psalm 139:23-24

I need to reboot this mind to restore and refresh my thinking according to God's Word. I can "save" and replace all the old files with the new ones made by Christ's love.

"The end of all things is near. Therefore be alert and of sober mind so that you may pray. Above all, love each other deeply, because love covers over a multitude of sins."
1 Peter 4:7-8

OPTIONS

There are only two options in this life: either we are a slave to sinful desires, or a servant of Christ. We are affected from birth by the choice our ancestors made, when Eve chose what appeared desirable to her, even though it was against God's command. And Adam followed her decision, into the perversion of our souls.

We have a nature that wants its own way, instead of what God says is good.

We do not realize the insidious thing that happens when we choose our own desires; we are giving control of our lives to an evil master. The enemy of all that is good, who opposes God, wants to control us and make us his puppet.

His ultimate goal is to separate us from the love of God, for eternity. He wants to subject us, as his captive, to the doom that is also his fate.

Under his influence, power-hungry people want to control us and make us do what they want. If we do not allow this subversion, they attempt to make us an example of the penalties they exact on those who won't concede to them. This is the way of the world, which is under the control of the evil one.

But we do not have to remain under his control; there is a way to freedom. Our sinful nature resists this idea, but freedom comes through complete surrender and submission to Christ. Letting go of yourself----- to Christ----- is the way to find your true self. It's a leap of faith.

You can trust the One who left the glory of Heaven, to be mistreated and crucified for your sake. This is the One who will never leave you or forsake you.

He will never deceive you; He is the way, the truth, and the life. He paid the tremendous price for your salvation.

Jesus' pledge to us of the fulfillment of all His promises is the gift of the Holy Spirit, which He will give to us when we surrender ourselves to Him.

The only safe place in this world is to be controlled by the Holy Spirit. Then we are no longer controlled by our desires or the evil one.

Every aspect of the Holy Spirit's personality is good, trustworthy, and faithful. Our lives are safe in His care, and our eternal destiny is assured, when we are following Him.

"Whoever sows to please their flesh, from the flesh will reap destruction; whoever sows to please the Spirit, from the Spirit will reap eternal life." Galatians 6:8

"For if you live according to the flesh, you will die; but if by the Spirit you put to death the misdeeds of the body, you will live. For those who are led by the Spirit of God are the children of God. The Spirit you received does not make you slaves, so that you live in fear again; rather, the Spirit you received brought about your adoption to sonship. And by him we cry, *"Abba,* Father." Romans 8:13-15

"Choose today whom you will serve." Joshua 24:15 NLT

RELENTLESS

A few nights ago during the worship time, we were singing about the relentless love of God.

It made me think of what we have to go through sometimes, before our stubborn hearts will yield to Him, and begin to pursue His love the way He longs for.

I thought of a Bible story.

This young man was not an exemplary character--far from it.

He cheated his own brother out of his inheritance and conspired with his mother to deceive his own father.

And we think our families have problems! This family became so full of strife and division that the young man had to flee for his life.

And then he met his uncle Laban, and "got a taste of his own medicine". It might have been like a mirror to see into the future----to see what he himself would become if he continued the way he was. Even his name---Jacob---meant "cheater".

His uncle Laban was all about cheating; he could not be trusted in any agreement made with him. His uncle pretended to care about him, so Jacob went to work for him. But Laban always found a way to deduct something from his wages, so that he didn't have to pay Jacob the full amount.

Jacob worked for him for seven years, for the privilege of marrying one of Laban's daughters. Jacob was in love with the younger daughter. However, on the wedding night,

Laban disguised the bride and gave Jacob the wrong daughter!

Jacob was stunned at the audacity of his uncle. But maybe he was ashamed, too, when he remembered that he had done a similar thing to his father and brother. He had disguised himself and pretended to be his brother in order to receive the birthright from their father.

Jacob could not undo what he had done; and he could not undo what was done to him. But he loved the younger daughter so much that he worked another seven years to have her for his wife. Now that is a true example of determination and patience!

Jacob had been away from home for many years. He never saw his mother again. Finally, the time came when Jacob realized he needed to leave and go home. He knew that Laban would never allow him to take what was rightfully his, so he would have to sneak away. So when the opportune time came, he did not hesitate. He and his wives and children left to go back to Jacob's homeland, with all that they possessed.

Laban was furious when he found out and pursued them, but he could not do anything to stop them and had to let them go.

But in regards to Jacob's brother Esau, who he had cheated, that was a different concern. As they drew closer to their homeland, Jacob's sentries found out that Esau was approaching with an army of 400 men.

That was a stressful day.

Jacob did his best to come up with a strategy to appease his brother, and save the lives of his family, but he was not sure if it was enough.

That night he met someone alone in the wilderness.

All this time, the Lord had been with Jacob, watching over him. Jacob was even given a vision of Heaven, with angels ascending and descending. The Lord blessed Jacob's work, even when Laban tried to rob him----and Jacob's flocks and herds---his wealth---increased.

But Jacob still only knew the Lord distantly.

That night, a Man came out of nowhere and began to wrestle with Jacob, when Jacob was alone with his fear-----of what might happen in the morning.

They wrestled through the night.

Jacob's hip was wrenched by the Man as they wrestled, but still he held on to the Man.

Then when it was almost morning, the Man said to Jacob, "Let me go." And Jacob answered, "I won't let you go until you bless me!" Jacob knew who this Man was---it was no man.

The Man asked him to identify himself, and Jacob told him his name was Jacob---the cheater. The Man answered, "Your name will no longer be Jacob. It will be Israel." Jacob's identity was changed----he became the man who struggled with God. And the Man blessed him.

Now Jacob had an intimate relationship with God; he became a seeker of God. He had struggled to pursue the Lord and received the blessing of a changed character.

The Lord is always watching over us, and blessing us so that we will notice Him. But He is waiting for the moment of crisis, when our stubborn self-reliance is broken and we can barely stand in our own strength.

If we cling to the Lord and won't let go, He will bless us! We will recognize Him at last, and He will change our identity and our destiny.

We will become seekers of God, who pursue Him to see His face and receive His blessing. And we will be given the family inheritance from our Heavenly Father.

This comes about because He is intent on pursuing us.

His love is relentless.

HIS THRONE

There have been many who have said recently, "God is still on the throne."

Yes, He is.

But to some with a particular perception of Him, this saying accentuates their impression of Him as a distant, cold, Supreme Being, whose only desire is to squash all resistance.

That is not who He is.

He wants to be close to us, but He will not violate our free will. We have to take the first step towards Him.

God is passionate in His love for us, and He is looking for those who will love Him passionately. It is His nature to give love.

The proof of this is seen in how He sent His Son into the world as a human, to make a way for us to have a relationship with Him.

We will not fully appreciate what happened at the Cross until we realize how much the Father passionately loves His Son, and how much the Son passionately loves His Father.

Their relationship existed before the creation of the world. They know what true love is; love was not created when the earth was formed.

Love was in existence long before that, because God is love.

When God gave to us the one He loved so much, it revealed His incomprehensible love. This reveals a love so great that our finite minds cannot fully comprehend it.

He wants you to accept it.....treasure it, and value it....as the greatest gift anyone has ever given. You cannot measure its value, but you can receive it.

His throne is the place of loving authority---the place from which His generous grace flows to us. His throne becomes a welcoming comforting thought instead of a repelling one.

When the world's culture tries to reduce our perception of Him to the level of the superstitious legends in its religions, we can be reassured that His truth will reign, when we remember His throne.

"The Lord has established his throne in heaven, and his kingdom rules over all." Psalm 103:19

Yes, the Lord is still on the throne.

"The Son is the radiance of God's glory and the exact representation of his being, sustaining all things by his powerful word. After he had provided purification for sins, he sat down at the right hand of the Majesty in heaven." Hebrews 1:3

PRICELESS

We could traverse the entire world and see its most famous wonders, from the Taj Mahal to the Northern Lights, and enjoy the most amazing of its entertainment venue---- and none of it could compare with the priceless joy of having the Lord speak to you----or being loved by Him in a personal, real way.

None of these temporal experiences could in any way come close in comparison, to the way the Lord speaks to us in an intimate way---or the way He lights up His Word in our minds, and reveals the intensity of the love with which He treasures us.

"When You said, "Seek My face," my heart said to You, "Your face, O LORD, I shall seek."" Psalm 27:8 NASB

"Seek the Lord and His strength; Seek His face continually." Psalm 105:4 NASB

The devil is afraid that one day we might find out who we are really meant to be.

He wants to keep us in the chicken yard, where our whole lives revolve around pecking, and pettiness.

We are meant to be eagles.

"But those who hope in the Lord will renew their strength. They will soar on wings like eagles; they will run and not grow weary, they will walk and not be faint." Isaiah 40:31

When we soar with Him, we can view the world from His perspective. When we seek Him-----we can fly.

THE ROYAL GUARD

Do you ever feel baffled? Overwhelmed and incompetent?

Anxious about your anxiety? Fearful about your fears?

Bewildered and confused?

Good.

Now you can experience God's peace---it's supernatural!!

We can't grasp it or understand it, but we don't need to.

All we have to do is this:

"Do not be anxious about anything, but in every situation, by prayer and petition, with thanksgiving, present your requests to God. And the peace of God, which transcends all understanding, will guard your hearts and your minds in Christ Jesus." Phil.4:6-7

We have a Personal Guard over our most vulnerable parts: our heart and mind.

Peace is standing guard. He will let you know what thoughts to let in. (Phil. 4:8)

So rejoice! Be gentle. The Lord is near.

Is He---

A far-away God? Never.

An uninvolved God? Hardly.

An indifferent God? Not at all.

An impotent powerless-to-act God? Absolutely not.

If you seek Him with all your heart, you will find Him.

He is waiting….until you want Him, and His sovereignty.

Then you will have the comfort of His peace as your Royal Guard.

It's beyond understanding.

"Lean on, trust in, and be confident in the Lord with all your heart and mind, and do not rely on your own insight or understanding." Proverbs 3:5 AMPC

UNIQUELY YOU

I really like to document events with photos. My tool is my camera.

I also love to celebrate people, with photography. I try to get a shot that will capture the beauty in that person and reveal it in a photo.

After each phase of His creation, God looked at it and He said it was good. On the seventh day, He rested----and I think that He not only stopped working, I think He took time to look at and enjoy and rejoice in all His wondrous creation.

I think He put that delight in us, too---after you work really hard, then you can rest and rejoice in the work He helped you to do. If you do your best for Jesus, you can be satisfied with the fruit of your labor. (Perfectionism, on the other hand, is discontent and never satisfied.)

We are His workmanship, and I believe He rejoices in us, even though the work is not finished yet. He will keep working on us until the day we cross over to His home.

Each of us is uniquely created by the Lord, and He cherishes His creation. The Scriptures tell us to accept one another as Christ accepts us. I don't think this means having an attitude that says "I accept your salvation, but I don't accept you as a person".

I think He means that He wants us to accept and appreciate each other as unique people, each one with special qualities. (Though I am NOT saying that we should accept blatant disregard for God's commands)

It's important that we replicate the Lord's character in this matter; that we show people His ways, as opposed to the old nature we had before we knew Christ.

The culture of the world in effect says, "I won't love you unless you conform to what I want." It's astounding how Jesus' standards are so opposite of the way the world's culture operates.

The world thinks that the peak of power, prestige, and status happens when people want to be your clone.

Jesus wants us to be the way He designed us to be---unique.

The world will hate us because we are not like them; it will hate us because we are different and will not conform to their culture. Our nature is changed and is becoming more like Christ's---we do not respond to the old standards or way of thinking.

If we continue to disdain people who are different from us, we are falling back into the old patterns and acting more like the world does, instead of the Kingdom of God.

Remember that it would be an insult to the Lord's artistry if we did not accept and value the uniqueness of each person. Acceptance of each other promotes the unity He desires.

We are His masterpiece; so celebrate His design! Appreciate the Lord's artistry.

Worship the Lord, and rejoice in each other.

Ephesians 2:10 Romans 15:7

THE NATURE OF GRACE

Jesus never despises a broken heart. He never looks down with disfavor on the weary. He has open arms for the broken-hearted, and the weary ones.

He has comfort for those who have been repressed and shunned, and He has strength for those who have been oppressed and abused.

He has healing for those who have been wounded and rejected. This is His nature----the nature of Grace.

But in order to receive these benefits, we also have to embrace another part of His nature---FORGIVENESS.

We can't be healed unless we forgive.

When Jesus hung there on the Roman cross dying, He said these words: "Father, forgive them, for they do not know what they are doing." Luke 23:34

Was He saying that the people who crucified Him were justified in what they did? Was He admitting that He conceded to their accusations? Was He saying that He assented and agreed with their opinions of Him?

No, He was not. True forgiveness does NOT condone wrong actions or excuse them. It does not call what is evil, good.

True forgiveness brings about concern and compassion for a person---despite the wrong they have done. True forgiveness shows mercy to people who do not deserve it. (And that is ALL of us) This is the nature of forgiveness.

This nature comes from Jesus; it is not in ours. We can only be like Him when He lives in us, and we accept all that He is.

We are forgiven, so we can forgive.

We MUST resist the enemy and his hateful ways---but NEVER put up a resistance when Jesus comes knocking at your door, wanting to fellowship with you. Open your heart to Him all the way. (Revelation 3:20)

"God resists the proud,
But gives grace to the humble." James 4:6 NKJV

UNDYING LOVE

The Last Supper had many symbolic references to a Jewish wedding ceremony. Jesus was pledging His agape, God-given love to His friends and faithful beloved followers before His death.

His enemy would be able to put Him to death on the cross because it was the Heavenly Father's plan, but the love of Jesus for His friends could not and cannot die. This love withstood Death, and all of the enemy's evil hordes.

When He rose again from the dead, He made sure His friends knew it. He made sure they knew that His love for them did not die, and never will.

When Jesus lives in us, we too will have undying love for His friends. This does not mean that we will be blind to each other's mistakes and flaws; otherwise how could we effectively pray for one another? Christ-like love sees the value and potential in every person, and wants to help them succeed in His plan for their lives.

Even when the rich young ruler loved his possessions too much and turned away from following Christ, Jesus looked at him and loved him. Mark 10:21 (I have always hoped that later this young man realized his mistake and decided to follow the Lord.)

When we take Communion, it serves as a reminder to us of the undying love that Jesus has for us. It is also a reminder to the Body of Christ that we are more than just body parts with a function; we are friends and family members of one another. We should treat each other as holy.

The Lord does not love us just for our usefulness, and then forget us. He loves us just as much when we are feeble and weakened by age or dire circumstances. He is our Guide until the end of our lives.

"For this God is our God for ever and ever; he will be our guide even to the end." Psalm 48:14

He will never leave us or forsake us. (Hebrews 13:5)

That is the kind of Friend He is.

This is His character that He wants to invest in us, so that we will care for one another and fulfill His desires.

His love never fails; it never gives up. His love "always protects, always trusts, always hopes, always perseveres." 1 Corinthians 13:7

Can anything in this world ever compare to His kind of love? Not ever.

Hold on to His love.

HEALTHY LIVING

Lord, we are Your body.

Free us of any restrictions in the flow of Your Life-giving blood.

Rid us of impurities so that every part can receive nourishment and encouragement.

Help us to think like You do, so we will move the way You intend.

Heal our eyes of stigmatism so that we don't see others through a stigma.

Make the passions of Your heart the rhythm of our lives.

Protect us from the loss of hearing of Your voice.

Keep us from internal injuries of despair and fear.

Give us discernment of the warning signs of cancer--- abnormal cells of enmity, envy, disrespect, and malice---that try to infiltrate and harm us.

Focus the laser light of Your Spirit on these malignant cells to destroy them.

Cover our wounds with the ointment of joy.

Grow in us Your merciful loving nature.

Let our knees bend freely in hopeful prayer.

Strengthen our feet to walk in Your purposes with endurance.

Deliver us of heavy burdens that affect our posture and confidence.

Anoint our hands to worship You, and to bless others.

Show us how to live by your health instructions found in Your Word---with kindness and forgiveness.

Teach us to exercise our faith and not become lazy.

Transform us into Your image of goodness.

With every breath, fill us to glorify You.

TRUE LOVE

God is holy.....and God is love.

When you put those together, you have a love which can be totally trusted. It is an unchanging absolutely faithful love----not in the slightest bit fickle or insincere.

There are no lies, no pretense, no cover-ups, no exaggeration, no false dealings to shock you, and no hidden motives. He is true love.

It's hard to conceive of a Person so pure and good. He deals with us tenderly, and only disciplines to protect us from the deceitfulness of sin.

Yes, sin is characterized by deceit. The nature of our age-old enemy is deception---the opposite of truth. He is still trying to destroy you with his lies, and his false accusations.

Sometimes humans are his unwitting agents, but it is spirits we are battling, not people. Forgive the people, and fight the spirits in prayer.

"For our struggle is not against flesh and blood, but against the rulers, against the authorities, against the powers of this dark world and against the spiritual forces of evil in the heavenly realms." Ephesians 6:12

The Scriptures tell us to test the spirits----see if it is anti-Christ---something opposite of Jesus. If it is unholy, unloving, and untruthful-----it is anti-Christ. 1 John 4

Anti-Christ will someday be embodied in a man, but right now it is a spirit at work in our world producing evil. We need discernment----and the gifts of the Spirit. (1 Corinthians 12:8-10)

Jesus is the Word of God---know Him through His Word. Recognize Him by His Word----He never contradicts Himself. There is nothing false in Him.

If we obey His Word, we will not be living a lie.

When Christ lives in us through faith, we will be full of His Word, and there will be no room for anything false. We can be His peacemakers. James 3:17-18

We work for peace when we help people be reconciled to God, through His Son Jesus. 2 Corinthians 5:18-20

OUTSIDE THE BOX

You are an extraordinary God.

You do not do ordinary things; You do the unexpected, the surprising things.

A virgin conceives; a star leads travelers to a particular house; the Son of God became a human baby! What will He think of next?

You are greater than anyone's imagination, and no one can keep You in their "box", or conform You to their ways.

If we try to confine Him to our box of ideals, we miss out on the exhilarating freedom of abandonment to His love, and the joy of intimate worship!

There is no satisfaction in trying to be in control; our security and our peace are found in surrender to Him.

Today, let's open up our lives to His Spirit even more, and let Him have His way!

He will give us His creative energy, and make possibilities out of the impossible. We will begin to see His plan unfold.

Nothing can deter His plan. How astonishing it is to be included in it!

"But the plans of the LORD stand firm forever, the purposes of his heart through all generations." Psalm 33:11

UPGRADE

This is a parable for all of us:

Jesus wants to live with you in your heart-house.
Remember that famous picture of Jesus knocking at the
door?

What an honor, that the King of Kings would want to live with
us!

He accepts you and cherishes you....but wherever He goes,
His grace makes things better. So get ready for some
changes.

If you want Jesus to establish permanent residency in your
heart, there are things you must allow Him to do.

He will get rid of those little monsters you think of as pets:
pet peeves, favoritism, and the tricky little foxes of deceit.

He will insist that you accept His friends and not shame them
as if they are enemies. His equation is this: If He is for them
and not against them, and He is in you, then you must not be
against them. (3 John)

The Lord's house should be a place of prayer----not a den of
thieves. If you want Him to dwell with you, you cannot steal
from people their sense of worth, or dispose of their
contributions as worthless.

I think this is why Jesus pointed out the poor widow who only
put in a few coins worth less than a penny. Jesus wanted
His disciples to see how He perceives value. Others would

have sneered at her offering, but in His eyes, this woman's gift was of great worth.

It does not please the Lord if we speak to any of His servants in a patronizing manner, or condescendingly, or in a depreciating way.

Our goal should be to bless others through prayer and increase their value and effectiveness.

We have to give up feeling threatened and intimidated if the Lord uses someone who is not in our little group. The disciples had to deal with this situation in Luke 9:49-50:

"Master," said John, "we saw someone driving out demons in your name and we tried to stop him, because he is not one of us." "Do not stop him," Jesus said. "for whoever is not against you is for you."

Moses and his helper Joshua also faced this, and this is how Moses reacted:

"A young man ran and told Moses, "Eldad and Medad are prophesying in the camp." Joshua son of Nun, who had been Moses' aide since youth, spoke up and said, "Moses, my lord, stop them!" But Moses replied, "Are you jealous for my sake? I wish that all the LORD's people were prophets and that the LORD would put his Spirit on them!" Numbers 11:27-29

Are you a junk collector----hoarding envy, anger, and malice? If it is heart trash, it has to go, so He can fill your house with rare and beautiful treasures. Ephesians 4:31

He is more concerned with the interior than the exterior, and He beautifies His people with His salvation. Psalm 194:4

"By wisdom a house is built, and through understanding it is established; through knowledge its rooms are filled with rare and beautiful treasures." Proverbs 24:3-5

It may feel at times as if He is turning your house upside down! He is; His ways are opposite of ours:

The way up is down.   Matthew 18:4

The way to life is through death.   1 Peter 2:24

The last will be first.   Matthew 20:16

The way forward is back.   Luke 14:10

The winners are the losers. Luke 9:24

Strength comes from weakness.   2 Corinthians 12:10

Surrender is the way to victory.   Luke 9:23

He knows what He is doing! So just be grateful. If you trust Him, your life and your actions will show that He is trustworthy.

"But Christ is faithful as the Son over God's house. And we are his house, if indeed we hold firmly to our confidence and the hope in which we glory." Hebrews 3:6

The enemy downgrades people; the Holy Spirit upgrades.

There is an available upgrade; will you allow the Holy Spirit to make changes to your domain?

When you see what He can do, I think you will be very satisfied.

THROUGH PAIN

Sometimes people give correct, clinical, Scripture based counsel---and yet it doesn't apply to every person's situation. There may be hidden things below the surface of the situation that they are unaware of; they may be relying merely on appearances.

Jesus knows the heart of the matter; these are the times when we need the supernatural discernment from the Holy Spirit that Jesus gives.

A deeper intuition may come from an excruciating experience with pain, because it drives us to a greater intimacy with the Man acquainted with grief. Isaiah 53:1-12

The Lord is making us like Himself, and sometimes He uses painful circumstances. There will be a reward for enduring through pain. Job said: "But he knows the way that I take; when he has tested me, I will come forth as gold." Job 23:10

The Lord seems to put His dedicated servants in the "crucible." When we come out of that, we will be on display for His glory.

Sometimes God's ways are past discovery---we can't figure out what He is doing or put it into a neatly labeled doctrinal "test tube."

"Oh, the depth of the riches of the wisdom and knowledge of God! How unsearchable his judgments, and his paths beyond tracing out!" Romans 11:33

Our observations are not concrete analysis, because He is bigger than our finite minds! "Who has known the mind of the Lord? Or who has been His counselor?" Romans 11:34

"For my thoughts are not your thoughts, neither are your ways my ways," declares the Lord. "As the heavens are higher than the earth, so are my ways higher than your ways and my thoughts than your thoughts." Isaiah 55:8-9

Job's friends thought they had God all figured out, and Job's situation too---but Job trusted God even when he didn't understand. He didn't allow his convictions to be tampered with by his friends, either. Neither should we allow our friends to intimidate our faith.

Job knew his affliction was not his fault, though his friends insisted that he was to blame. Job was already a man who sought God and lived a life of repentance and obedience.

Job was not a perfect man; he expressed anger and frustration in his turmoil, but he could hear and recognize God's voice. Job desperately wanted to hear from the Lord, and when God spoke, Job listened-----and was changed by this encounter. He became more aware of the Lord's power and glory.

Job's friends' statements were false due to the perplexity of the situation, and they bombarded him with accusations. But Job held no grudges against them, and the Lord enlisted Job to intercede for them.

After that, the Lord began to restore everything the enemy had been allowed to steal from Job. And the restoration was greater than the loss!

People rejoiced to see the goodness of God when this happened. The Lord's character was vindicated, and people respected Job for his endurance.

The way through pain is difficult to understand, but Jesus has gone through it and knows the way. Hold onto Him and follow Him, and you will come through to your reward---His blessing on your life. Your testimony will minister to many.

Jesus is the way, the truth, and the life. John 14:6

His is the only true way; there is no other.

"Salvation is found in no one else, for there is no other name under heaven given to mankind by which we must be saved." Acts 4:12

A WAY OF SEEING

"The Lord will rescue his servants; no one who takes refuge in him will be condemned." Psalm 34:22 This verse holds so much reassurance for our hearts to relish.

But then the enemy tries to add to God's Word with "yes, but...." Or "only if....."

I think the enemy of our souls tries to make us think that there are "hidden clauses" in God's Word that limit the truth and application of it----that is, "fine print" that disqualifies us from receiving the benefit of God's promises. This enemy wants to nullify our hope.

The enemy of God's truth creates distrust by hinting that there are invisible restrictions in God's Word which will eliminate you in the end.

The Lord does require heart-felt and love-motivated obedience to His Word and the guidance of the Holy Spirit. We are kept safe by following the Lord's directions.

But there are no "hidden clauses" to exclude us from His benefits.

The enemy makes a very poor lawyer when he contrives to use God's own truth to shut us out from God's mercy. The enemy's method and motive is condemnation by trying to convince us that God's promises are unattainable due to many stipulations.

The Lord is for us, not against us. This means He does NOT want you to fail. He is not setting up "roadblocks" to make it harder for you to reach Him.

He is not indifferent and casual about your progress. If He says something, He means it; it is not an advertising slogan to persuade you.

Don't listen if the enemy tries to make you feel that the Lord has an elite group He chooses, and you're not in it. Pray for vision to "see" what God actually says.

The enemy would like us to feel that humility means having a lack of confidence that we are right with God. This deceptive fiend wants us to feel constantly insecure and unsure about our acceptance by God, and to be weighed down by our lack.

These and other similar attitudes are actually "religious" thoughts that will make us self-centered instead of God-centered. A person without confidence focuses on his own insecurities rather than the needs of others. Insecurity is not humility.

On the other side of the spectrum are those who have mistakenly believed that the only way to be strong is to be harsh, critical, domineering, and judgmental. This is also a deviation from the truth of God's Word.

The goal is to develop a deep, deep trust in the Lord's love for us----and to REALLY believe what He says. Our faith pleases God. Hebrews 11:6

MIRACLES

I am a nobody---but He, the Lord of all creation, hears my voice when I call.

I am a person of little consequence---but He, the Ruler over all, answers my prayer.

I am a tiny bit of dust on a tiny little planet---but He, the King of this universe, knows my name.

He knows my thoughts before I think them.

He knows how many hairs are on my head!

He sees me, and includes me in His plans.

He has strong arms and a gentle heart and He loves me.

This is grace----He is gracious beyond all comprehension----to someone like me.

Incredible as it sounds, He has endowed me with eternal life.

And He will do all this for you, too.

I think we have grown accustomed to that phrase "eternal life"----so familiar with it, that we don't see the miracle.

But it is the most tremendous miracle we will ever experience.

It is the greatest destiny we could ever have.

He planned this before He ever created the world, because of His mercy.

Don't let yourself be cheated out of what He has specifically planned for you.

There is no substitute for a love like this.

He says, "Come to me, all you who are weary and burdened, and I will give you rest. Take my yoke upon you and learn from me, for I am gentle and humble in heart, and you will find rest for your souls." Matthew 11:28-29

This is Jesus----this is who He is.

The King who rules the universe cares about us.

He is the True Friend who will never forsake us.

If we want to know Him in this way, we need to trust Him with our lives.

It is not enough to believe that He exists----even demons can do that. When you come to Him in trust, and yield to His ways, you will find the kind of rest that revitalizes the soul.

LETTERS

A sweet friend recently gave me a letter expressing gratitude, and it meant a great deal to me. Letters can be so special.

2 Corinthians 3:3 says, "You show that you are a letter from Christ...."

In the version called the Voice, the whole verse reads like this:

"You are the living letter of the Anointed One, the Liberating King, nurtured by us and inscribed, not with ink, but with the Spirit of the living God---a letter too passionate to be chiseled onto stone tablets, but emblazoned upon the human heart."

It will take God's glory to become Living Epistles.....living letters.

Let us make our homes into a dwelling place for the Lord's glory, and when we go to His house to meet with other believers, let us bring His glory with us.

The former things will be like nothing compared to the glory He wants to send.

We have only begun to glimpse His power and His glory.

Psalm 63:1-8

"You, God, are my God, earnestly I seek you;
I thirst for you, my whole being longs for you,
in a dry and parched land where there is no water.

I have seen you in the sanctuary and beheld your power and your glory.
Because your love is better than life, my lips will glorify you.
I will praise you as long as I live, and in your name I will lift up my hands.
I will be fully satisfied as with the richest of foods; with singing lips my mouth will praise you.

On my bed I remember you; I think of you through the watches of the night.
Because you are my help, I sing in the shadow of your wings.
I cling to you; your right hand upholds me."

I can't please God-----at least, not in myself. There is nothing good enough in me.

So I am clinging to the only sinless One who can: Jesus.

Peter heard God's voice coming out of heaven on the mountain, and God said: "This is my Son, whom I love; with him I am well pleased." 2 Peter 1:17-18

There on the mountain with Jesus, Peter got a glimpse of the glory of God!

I will cling to Jesus and stay as close as possible---even in His "shadow". Then when the Father looks my way, He will see me through Jesus. Jesus will be the filter He looks through, and God the Father will be pleased. If we walk with Him, I know we will see His glory.

BEAST AND THE BEAUTY

I'm sure you have heard of the fairy tale about the enchanted prince who has become a beast---he must make a beautiful girl love him for his self to be free of the curse.

Recently we watched the 1987 film version of the tale, and it made me think of my Prince.

In my own version the prince is not the one under a curse---it was me.

I am the beast.

I am the one so ugly with sin that I did not think the Prince would love me.

But He said, "I do. Will you marry Me and become part of My bride?"

And He says, "The more you look into the mirror of My word, and see me as I really am, you will be changed into My beauty."

The more I look at Him in His Word, and see how beautiful He truly is, the more I am changed into His likeness.

The curse has been broken because of His sacrifice of Himself on the cross. There could not be a clearer example of His love.

He did this because He wants me----and you----to know Him, and be with Him.

He wants us to love Him back----not for His favors, or what He produces----but for who He is.

He doesn't just love us for what our lives can produce or for what we do for His kingdom; He loves us for ourselves.

He doesn't want people to simply believe that He exists; He wants us to believe in His good character. He wants us to trust Him----that He is a faithful Friend who will never leave us.

He is right now preparing a place for us in His Father's home.

He is faithful and true to His word----always.

"But we all, with unveiled face, beholding as in a mirror the glory of the Lord, are being transformed into the same image from glory to glory, just as from the Lord, the Spirit." 2 Corinthians 3:18 NASB

"So foolish, stupid, and brutish was I, and ignorant; I was like a beast before You." Psalm 73:22 AMPC

"I ask only one thing from the Lord. This is what I want: Let me live in the Lord's house all my life. Let me see the Lord's beauty...." Psalm 27:4 NCV

IN THE STARS

Sometimes the Gospel may seem like a fairy tale to us because we can't comprehend how God could possibly have an intimate relationship with every single person who has ever lived on this planet or who ever will.

Yet creation itself reveals the answer to this dilemma; the universe is so vast that we don't know where it ends----and it is still expanding.

The invisible attributes of God are visible through the marvel of His creation. The Scriptures tell us that He numbers the stars, and calls them each by name. Psalm 147:4

Scientists don't know how many stars are out there in this universe; it would be impossible to count them. But the Lord has a name for each one. Nothing is impossible for this great God.

We are without excuse if we think there is not enough evidence to prove His existence. Romans 1:20

Every human baby that is born into this world is a divine miracle of His creation. The more that science reveals the complexity of the human cell and the miracle of DNA, the more irrefutable it is that God exists......and that He designed us.

If He designed us, that means He has a plan for us. It is not a plan to destroy us.

He proved this when He sent His only Son into the world as a human to rescue us.

BELIEVE

Faith is credited as righteousness. Faith leads to obedience.

Abraham believed though he had never seen God; he believed in His voice, and he obeyed when the Lord told him to journey to a new land that he had never seen.

There is also an invisible enemy who DOES want to destroy you.

Jesus shed His blood to prevent your destruction.....if you will BELIEVE.

When the enemy comes at you, and tells you that there is no way that Jesus could love someone like you, you can answer back with all the authority of Heaven:

"Oh, yes He does and His shed blood proves it!!" That is what makes the blood of Jesus so powerful---it is PROOF that Jesus loves us!

The enemy cannot hold us hostage with discouragement from lies and accusations. He has no legal argument against the blood of Jesus. NONE.

Revelations 1:5 "To him who loves us and has freed us from our sins by his blood"

His blood will never lose its power.

TREASURE

God's Word is not wishful thinking.

His declarations cannot be revoked or rescinded.

Man's opinions cannot alter His truth.

His Word goes forth in power, and nothing can stop it or hinder what He says.

It will accomplish His purposes, and produce.

When planted in our lives, it grows, because His words have life in them.

It will grow eternal things in us----that is the kind of life His word possesses.

"I rejoice in your word like one who discovers a great treasure." Psalm 119:162 NLT

His Word is our greatest national treasure.

Yet for many, it lies forgotten---buried under a heap of rubble.

It lies hidden under a huge pile of worthless words and trash thoughts.

The situation is similar to the time in history when Josiah became king in Israel.

At that time, the house of God was in disrepair, and the Word of God had become lost.

When they finally found it, they realized how much it had been neglected, and how polluted their nation had become because of this.

Renewal cannot come without repentance---we have to recognize our need.

And we need to recognize the tremendous value there is in obedience to God's Word.

It is not a magic formula that we apply to our situations in order to find relief.

The Word of God is supernatural----it must be believed and obeyed. There is an action required of us because the scriptures are the eternal promises of God.

We obey because we believe in the absolute authority of God.

When we do this, we will see supernatural things happen.

This is His promise.

NO SEPARATION

"Therefore what God has joined together, let no one separate." Mark 10:9

I used to think of this only in terms of human marriage. But we are the Bride of Christ. Jesus does not want us to allow any person to separate us from Him-----or from each other.

He does not want us to allow anything to corrupt our love for Him or for each other.

Where does corruption in this world come from?

It comes from evil desires----the human heart has evil desires because it is self-centered. It wants what it wants, no matter what.

God has given us His great promises to escape the corruption in the world caused by evil desires. These are the Heaven-breathed, Spirit empowered words of truth that can show the difference between what is from human desire, and what is born of the Spirit.

"Through these he has given us his very great and precious promises, so that through them you may participate in the divine nature, having escaped the corruption in the world caused by evil desires." 2 Peter 1:4

"For the word of God is alive and active. Sharper than any double-edged sword, it penetrates even to dividing soul and spirit, joints and marrow; it judges the thoughts and attitudes of the heart." Hebrews 4:12

Like a bride yearns for her bridegroom, we are meant to yearn for intimacy with Jesus through the Holy Spirit. Our desire should be for Him---to be with Him.

"Whom have I in heaven but you? And earth has nothing I desire besides you." Psalm 73:25

And out of that intimacy, things are created in us by the Spirit; things are produced from our lives that can only be born of the Spirit and not by human endeavor. This is where true ministry comes from.

"Take delight in the Lord, and he will give you the desires of your heart." Psalm 37:4

This is not a "magic formula" to get what you want from the Lord. If you take delight in the Lord, it speaks of an intimate relationship-----one that will change all your desires.

If you "delight yourself in the Lord", that means He is your passion, the One you crave with all your heart........your delight is not religious authority and power, not position in the church, not popularity, not status, not prestige. All you want is to be filled with His love and truth, and to have this flow out of you because it is what He wants.

Oh, Lord, may we continually desire this intimacy with You.....and make us one in the Spirit, joined together by Your love. Help us to fight against all that opposes this intimacy and would drive us apart. Let no one separate what God has joined together.

UP CLOSE AND PERSONAL

On Easter Sunday afternoon I was helping our three year old granddaughter with her Beginners Bible Easter story sticker book. Two adjacent pages had pictures of Jesus' tomb. One picture showed the tomb sealed up with the stone, and had a place for 2 stickers of Roman soldiers standing in front of the tomb. Ruby put an angel sticker on top of the tomb.

The other picture showed a close-up view of the tomb with the stone rolled away, the same angel sitting on the stone, and the 2 soldiers lying down on the ground.

The first picture's viewpoint was from a distance, and in the second one, the figures were much larger since it was a close-up view.

Ruby looked at the first picture and said, "This is a little angel." And I said, "Actually the two angels are the same size. It just depends on where you are standing when you look at the tomb."

This morning I realized what an enormous concept perspective must be for a young child who is just learning spatial comparisons of objects! At this age, they are just learning the concept of "big" and "little" with 2 similar objects. I don't know if Ruby was able to grasp the idea of perspective.

And sometimes we adults too have a difficult time "putting things into perspective."

When you are far away from the truth of Jesus' resurrection, the whole thing seems "small" and petty. You will not be able to realize the enormity of these events when you remain distant.

Some people purposely present a perspective that makes Jesus look "small." They try to bring Him down to a human level and downplay His divinity and sinless nature----so that they will not have to surrender or submit to Him.

They want a "small" perspective so they can stay far away from Him and His truth.

You will only find out how magnificent He is when you are willing to come close and allow His story to become personal to you. Then you can see the immense magnitude of the Resurrection.

Your perspective will change and you will no longer have a small-minded, narrowly focused viewpoint. Jesus expands your horizon from colloquial and commonplace to Heavenly.

This world is no longer just a playground to you; it becomes a launching point into Eternity----and into the vast expanse of God's grace.

The Resurrection exhibits a power greater than any other, and unlike anything in this world.

The Lord says in Isaiah 33:13: "You who are far away, hear what I have done; you who are near, acknowledge my power!" "Come near to God and he will come near to you." is the promise found in James 4:8.

"The Lord is near to all who call on him, to all who call on him in truth." Psalm 145:18

"let us draw near to God with a sincere heart and with the full assurance that faith brings...." Hebrews 10:22

FEAR DRIVES

So many times, people hurt other people because we are all so afraid....we hurt people in an effort to protect ourselves. Fear drives us to hurt one another.

When we are not trusting the Lord to protect us, there occurs a natural human reaction to "lash out" and exact revenge and attack people verbally as a means of self-protection.

The opposite of fear is trust. "When I am afraid, I put my trust in you." Psalm 56:3

"Perfect love drives out fear" 1 John 4:18 If we allow His perfect love to fill us, it will drive out fear and keep us from hurting people out of self-protection.

It's a dog-eat-dog culture, and fear motivates aggression; we subconsciously think we will be safe if we practice domination through aggression. Without trust, we think we can control our environment through our own efforts.

The Lord redeems our lives from destruction. Psalm 103:4

"At one time we too were foolish, disobedient, deceived and enslaved by all kinds of passions and pleasures. We lived in malice and envy, being hated and hating one another. But when the kindness and love of God our Savior appeared, he saved us, not because of righteous things we had done, but because of his mercy." Titus 3:3-5

Take a step of faith and trust; take the first step as a peacemaker. Nothing good comes from holding grudges or fighting for one's rights at the expense of relationship.

This is what Christ showed us; He did not hold onto His rights as King of this universe, but took on the form of a servant. He humbled Himself even to die a criminal's death on the Cross. Philippians 2:5-8

He made peace between us and God the Father by means of His own blood. He did this for the sake of having a relationship with us. Ephesians 2:13

Following Him is not easy when He asks us to do what we don't want to do. Pride comes naturally to us; humility does not. Luke 9:23

But this is what He means when He said, "Take up your cross." It means deny yourself the privilege of "rights" over relationship; it means allow yourself NO grudges, only forgiveness. Ephesians 4:32

It means consider others over yourself; consider how you can edify that person, and encourage them, and act on it. It takes courage and integrity of heart, but it is the path of Mercy. 1 Thessalonians 5:11

The Lord wants us to love Mercy, because it is so much of who He is.

"He has shown you, O mortal, what is good. And what does the Lord require of you? To act justly and to love mercy and to walk humbly with your God." Micah 6:8

THE PRINCE

He was raised by a princess, who found him floating in the river and rescued him. She took him out of the water and named him Moses.

He was raised in the palace, though his people were the slaves who built the monumental edifices of the king. He saw the conditions that the slaves were subject to, as they worked.

When he was grown, he could not ignore the injustice that he witnessed. Perhaps he felt that he was in a position to be the savior of his people, so he acted as a vigilante-----he defended a slave by killing the taskmaster.

When his actions were discovered, he found out that he was not considered a hero, but a criminal. He was no match for the world's greatest political power. So he fled into the wilderness, and disappeared.

He spent 40 years in the wilderness with nomads, learning the life of a shepherd. His life as an Egyptian prince was a very distant memory, and I'm sure he had no intention of going back----until God called to him out of a burning bush.

What happened during those forty years? I think a lot of the effect of Egyptian culture had to be removed from his mind, so that he could hear God's call. He began a relationship with the Lord that he considered to be worth more than all the treasures of Egypt.

He did become the deliverer for his people----though not at all in the way that he had thought. The exodus of the slaves from Egypt came after the greatest display of God's power that the world had ever seen.

I think there were some who joined the Exodus because they wanted to be in on a good thing, and this God sure had power! I don't think they were certain that He was completely trustworthy, however, so at the first sign of difficulty, they began to wonder what kind of God He was. They complained and doubted His good intentions. When you really believe in someone, you trust their motives and desires. They were not sure about this God because of the troubles they faced, so they turned against Him and made an idol.

Moses and the Lord had a heart-to-heart talk about this situation. The Lord said to Moses, "I have seen this people, and they are a stiff-necked people indeed! Let me alone, so that I may destroy them and blot out their name from under heaven. And I will make you into a nation stronger and more numerous than they." Deuteronomy 9:13-14.

If Moses had been a different person, this might have been a tempting offer. These people had given Moses nothing but trouble since the day they left Egypt. They grumbled, complained, and often blamed Moses. I can see how Moses could have desired to be free of these stubborn people, and start over with new people. And some would have been delighted to have a nation named after themselves, and a legacy as great as God described.

Moses was not enticed. He wasn't thinking of himself at all; he was thinking of how this would affect the way people thought of God. Moses was more concerned for the Lord's reputation than his own.

This is how he responded: "Sovereign LORD, do not destroy your people, your own inheritance that you redeemed by your great power and brought out of Egypt with a mighty hand. Remember your servants Abraham, Isaac and Jacob. Overlook the stubbornness of this people, their wickedness and their sin. Otherwise, the country from which you brought us will say, 'Because the LORD was not able to take them into the land he had promised them, and because he hated them, he brought them out to put them to death in the wilderness.'" Deuteronomy 9:26-28

Moses truly believed in the Lord----in the Lord's character---and believed that He was totally trustworthy. And I think that because of this, the Lord trusted in Moses. It was a true friendship between them that I admire.

I believe that the Lord knew what Moses' response would be, and that he would petition for the people to be spared. And because of the Lord's merciful character, I believe He was pleased with this. This was the kind of leader the Lord could trust.

Moses cared about God's glory and honor more than his own, and he stayed in a situation that was often very stressful, and with people who were hard to deal with, because it would bring more honor to the Lord than giving up on them.

Moses spent another forty years in the wilderness, leading and guiding and teaching the people of the Exodus.

Years later, we get a glimpse of the ongoing friendship between the Lord and Moses. Elijah and Moses were seen by the first disciples of Jesus. Elijah and Moses had been in Heaven for many years, but they appeared in their heavenly forms and were having a discussion with Jesus about future events. Matthew 17:1-3

Moses and the Lord were still having heart-to-heart talks!

The best part of this story is in knowing that we can have this kind of relationship with the Lord, too.

You don't need to wait until you see a bush on fire, either.

ETERNITY IN OUR HEARTS

I am only a bunch of dust particles....but Your Spirit gives me Life.

You have put eternity in our hearts. Ecclesiastes 3:11 The body will return to dust, but part of me is joined to You for eternity and will never die.

When you are young, you feel immortal and brazen enough to think you are---but it is an illusion. As you age, you begin to understand that we are all slowly dying.

But if we "abide in Jesus", we will produce fruit that will remain. John 15:5 NKJV

The story of Jesus, and how His story changed us, and our testimony of this, will live on.

Whoever is in the headlines now will not be remembered, but whatever you do for Christ will be in His Story---the REAL HISTORY---for eternity.

Your life is a very valuable thing; it is a gift from God. Don't waste it----don't spend it on worthless things.

Nothing else will outlast our lives except what is done for the Lord's sake and His Kingdom. Nothing else has lasting value.

What is impressive in this world may be worth nothing in His. Are you only working behind the scenes? It's not a bad place to be; it's usually where God is working, though many times His kindness goes unnoticed.

You are the steward of your life; it is not your own, but you are responsible for your choices as the manager of God's property. Christ paid for your life with His life; He redeemed your life from destruction. His blood was the ransom to save you from eternal death.

So it is not ours to choose how to spend. He has a plan--- and He designed us to fit His plan. Nothing but His plans will be a perfect fit.

In this life, there are many changes. But God does not---He never changes. He is the Constant One who remains the same yesterday, today, and forever.

He is the Eternal One, and His Word endures beyond all dimensions of time and space. Yet He has plans for us--- though we are only dust.

God looked into the future and knew what would happen---- He knew of Adam and Eve's choice and Lucifer's rebellion. He saw it all---He saw the sacrifice of His Son in the future.

Yet He created us with that foreknowledge of our downfall. Why? So that people would love Him more after the fall and the sacrifice of His Son?

No, He looked into the future and He loved you, and He wanted you to have life. The enemy still tries to make us think of God as someone who will take from us, deny us, and exploit us. The opposite is true; God is a Giver, not a Taker.

He gives ETERNAL LIFE.

SONLIGHT

Our hearts are lonely for God's presence like plants long for the sunshine.

But there IS a battle to get into God's presence---the old carnal nature doesn't want to, and the enemy sure doesn't want this----he resists everything good.

Yet our hearts will never be happy without it.

We cannot grow into what we are meant to be without it.

Are you insecure and lack confidence in yourself?

Do you have the torment of fear swirling around in your mind?

Do you face obstacles of criticism and belittling prejudice?

Does anger try to overtake you and stifle love?

Are you frustrated over what you can't control or fix?

We lack much.....but God doesn't.

The answer to what we need is in His presence.

That's what Jesus has been trying to tell us.

The power of His Spirit is what we need.

IT'S SUPERNATURAL

The Kingdom of God is a supernatural invisible Kingdom. It's high above the traditions and customs and ways of this world and the perceptions of earthly systems.

It is not fantasy, or magic---just a different reality. You cannot see the Holy Spirit, but like the wind, you can see what He does. He is like the primary agent of the Kingdom of God.

"Jesus answered, Very truly I tell you, no one can enter the kingdom of God unless they are born of water and the Spirit. Flesh gives birth to flesh, but the Spirit gives birth to spirit."

"You should not be surprised at my saying, 'You must be born again.' The wind blows wherever it pleases. You hear its sound, but you cannot tell where it comes from or where it is going. So it is with everyone born of the Spirit." John 3:5-8

That is why the natural man cannot understand the truths of the Kingdom of God----they sound foolish to the natural mind.

"But a natural man does not accept the things of the Spirit of God, for they are foolishness to him; and he cannot understand them, because they are spiritually appraised."
1 Corinthians 2:14 NASB

If we are not seeking to live in the Supernatural, it is most likely that we are living in the Superficial.

"So I tell you: Live by following the Spirit. Then you will not do what your sinful selves want." Galatians 5:16 NCV

This is where I want to live; in the reality of the Kingdom of God.

Focus on the Lord.....His love, His power, His Word, His goodness, His grace.

"But seek first the kingdom of God and His righteousness..." Matthew 6:33 NKJV

This is the remedy for our malady----our sin induced minds and hearts.

The Lord gives us more of His Holy Spirit if we ask Him, to enable us to see His invisible Kingdom, and to live in the supernatural ways of the Holy Spirit.

The more I see, the more I realize I need to see more.

"My eyes are ever on the Lord..." Psalm 25:15

DO NOT FEAR

Heaven holds no fear; so beings from that place do not fear. In almost every angelic encounter with human beings, their message begins with "Do not fear." Fear is abnormal to Heaven and its inhabitants.

At the time of Jesus' birth, some shepherds out in the fields near Bethlehem saw an angel in the sky and they were terrified. "But the angel said to them, "Do not be afraid." Luke 2:10

When Jesus was with His disciples in a boat out on the Sea of Galilee, and they were in the midst of a deadly storm, the disciples cried out in fear. Jesus had been sleeping, but He woke up at the sound of their fear. He got up and commanded the wind and the waves, and they became still. Then He turned to the disciples and said, "Why are you so afraid?" He didn't punish them for their fear; He didn't say: "Because you were afraid, I'm going to make you suffer in this storm longer." He stopped the storm. I think He wanted them to realize that fear does not belong where He is. (This account is found in Mark 4:35-40.)

Peter, James, and John got a glimpse of heavenly glory up on the mountain with Jesus, but it was so awesome and powerful, that they fell down in fear. Jesus touched them and said, "Don't be afraid." (Matthew 17:6-7)

When John saw Jesus in the vision of Revelations, John fell down as if dead. But Jesus put His right hand on John and said, "Do not be afraid." (Revelation 1:17)

Fear is something the enemy interjected into this world because he delights in tormenting, intimidating, and taking people captive.

You will not find fear in Heaven. You will find perfect love, and perfect love drives out fear.

"There is no fear in love. But perfect love drives out fear, because fear has to do with punishment. The one who fears is not made perfect in love." 1 John 4:18

Whenever there is a spirit that wants to dominate others through fear or intimidation, it is not of God. The enemy lusts for power to rule, and uses aggression to cause fear.

"The fear of the Lord is the beginning of wisdom..." Proverbs 9:10 The "fear" in this verse means a deeply felt reverence, awe, and respect that will lead to obedience out of love and gratitude and unfeigned trust.

When the Scriptures teach us to "fear" God, it does not mean the tormenting intimidating fear found in this world.

There is only one instance in which you should be afraid of God, and that is if you are rebelling against His love and authority. That rebellion puts you on the same side as the fallen angels (demons) who rebelled against God. They are afraid---and for good reason---they shudder and tremble at the thought of God's coming judgement.

The Lord is the Good Shepherd---He does not want His flock to be tormented by fear. He says to us, "Do not be afraid, little flock, for your Father has been pleased to give you the kingdom." Luke 12:32 If you are trusting in Him, there is no reason to fear.

IN PRAISE

Are you in a prison? A place of despair and discouragement and disappointment that you never thought you would be in?

Faith will break you out. Begin to sing in the dark.

Praise the Lord in the gloom. Worship Him despite your pain.

Your chains will fall off, and your heart will be set free.

Don't destroy yourself---there is a name by which you are saved.

"Everyone who calls on the name of the Lord will be saved" Rom. 10:13 No Exceptions!!

Yes, we may have to suffer in this world because evil is so rampant that people cannot recognize what is good.

But when you worship, prison walls shake, and the Light will come. People will tremble in the light, but they will listen to the Truth.

Whole families will be brought into the Kingdom of Christ.

And your wounds will be healed.

You will fellowship in joy with new believers.

This is what happened to Paul and Silas and the jailer in the Philippian jail. Acts 16:16-34

It happened in the visible "natural" world to them; I believe it can happen in the unseen spiritual realm in our lives.

GUARDIANS OF THE GALAXY

We watched the movie by that name, and found out why it is so appealing. The movie is about a group of "misfits"---an unlikely band of heroes who don't even like each other at first. Eventually, a bond between them forms as they battle evil together.

Sometimes we don't realize who we really are as believers in Christ. We are armor-bearers; we are guardians of the church. (By church, I mean the group of believers we worship with) We are meant to nurture, intercede for, and "look out" for other believers in our local church. We should especially remember to pray for our leaders---for direction, anointing, and protection.

When you begin to operate in this role, the enemy may try to "take you out" to lower the defenses of the church. He may even try to use "friendly fire" to do his evil, and destroy you.

But the Lord's purposes remain firm. We remain "Guardians of the Galaxy." Our weapons are not of this world, but they have power to demolish strongholds. (2 Corinthians 10:4)

We are not of this world; we are aliens and temporary residents. Our citizenship is in another world. We haven't yet seen the fulfillment of God's promises----they won't all be fulfilled in this world. We are pilgrims just passing through. Hebrews 11:13

But when we go through dry places or places of grief, we make it a place of pools----an oasis in the wilderness. We go from blessing to blessing----from strength to strength.

"Blessed are those whose strength is in you, whose hearts are set on pilgrimage. As they pass through the Valley of Baka, they make it a place of springs; the autumn rains also cover it with pools. They go from strength to strength, till each appears before God in Zion." Psalm 84:5-7

We are living supernatural lives through faith. Faith that is seen or realized is not faith; faith is the state of believing in the unseen reality. Hebrews 11:1 We battle in faith and prayer.

Sometimes we are restless and we don't know why. It's because we can't "settle down" here. We are made for more. Our hope is not on earth or in earthly things, nor in its power struggles, lust for fame, or its greed and aggression. Hebrews 11:16

When our King---the King of the Universe---calls our name, we will go up to meet Him! That mighty shout could be all of our names put together. (The Bible doesn't say what He shouts, but nothing is impossible for Him----He has no limits) 1 Thessalonians 4:16-17

Until then, be guardians together of the galaxy----stay engaged in the battle against evil.

Keep the high praises of God in your mouth, and a sharp, double-edged sword in your hand. Psalm 149:6 That double-edged sword is the Word of God. Hebrews 4:12

"Be on your guard; stand firm in the faith; be courageous; be strong." 1 Corinthians 16:13

"Fight the good fight of the faith." 1 Timothy 6:12 Contend for the faith. Jude 1:3

THE HIGHEST AIM

One Sunday morning, the Lord said to me in the service,

"DON'T PRESUME TO BE RIGHTEOUS WITHOUT MY LOVE."

It didn't seem as if He was speaking to me personally, but to all of us. Yet it didn't come as a prophecy; so I wrote it down, thought about it and prayed about it.

These are the thoughts that came to me concerning this message:

We can be fear-driven; or we can be love-driven.

"For Christ's love compels us, because we are convinced that one died for all, and therefore all died." 2 Corinthians 5:14

We can do NOTHING without Christ's love, compassion, and mercy filling, leading and motivating us.

There IS no righteousness without Christ's love---therefore we cannot do anything Right without being filled with His love.

Righteousness is not present without the Lord's presence.

Without a relationship with Him, we can never be righteous.

That's why He tells us to remain in Him. Apart from Him, we can do NOTHING. John 15:5

Without His love, we are merely the noise of clanging symbols. 1 Corinthians 13:1

The root of bitterness will choke out love----pull it out. Destroy it before it corrupts love. Hebrews 12:15

It is the love of Christ that makes us holy and keeps us holy. The standard of righteousness is His love.

Over all other virtues, put on His love----His love holds it all together. Colossians 3:14

Christ's love is the highest aim of godly goals----it's on top. 2 Peter 1:5-7

Success = living in Christ's love. 2 Peter 1:8

This is the way to be productive and effective in God's Kingdom.

Love who and what He loves. Ephesians 5:1

Treat everyone as the objects of His love.

DESTINY

"Enter through the narrow gate. For wide is the gate and broad is the road that leads to destruction, and many enter through it. But small is the gate and narrow the road that leads to life, and only a few find it." Matthew 7:13-14

The wide road is well populated because it is popular.

The narrow road doesn't look very appealing because not many are on it, and some of these are.....well, misfits.....and peculiar people.....and that's kind of embarrassing.

We should not gravitate to whatever is popular or looks appealing. It would be far better to travel with some "misfits" than to end up on the road to destruction!

The road to choose is a narrow road because these people have narrowed their Authority for Truth to one source: God's Word.

If we find ourselves accepting what the culture says as truth, then we have strayed from the narrow road and we are not going to the right destination.

Our ultimate destination----our destiny----is what is most important.

So we have to be careful not to just follow everybody else---- we must make sure we know where we are going.

The destiny on the wide popular road is destruction. Our destiny on the narrow road is life; this is what Jesus said.

If we doubt what He says, it means we have been listening to the one who always tries to instill doubt about what God says.

It's how he deceived the human race in the First Place-----the Garden of Eden.

Don't reject what God says; reject what the enemy says.

God wants to help us; the enemy wants to harm us.

We will be safe in the Lord's care on the narrow road; He will look after us. And some of those misfits may turn out to be very wise people indeed, after we know them better.

Best of all, we will get to know Jesus better----His presence is with us on the narrow road. There is no better traveling companion than He is! He is our personal guide on the narrow road, who will escort us to our destiny in this life and beyond.

He not only knows the way, He IS the way.

BROKEN

The Heavenly Father allowed His beloved Son to be rejected and wounded----for our sakes. (Isaiah 53) People denounced Him and treated Him as if He were an evil person.

And sometimes, I think He may allow us to be rejected and wounded for the sake of others.

In those times, we need to remember how much the Father loves us, and that He is not punishing us for something we did, or didn't do.

We have to trust that His purposes are for good; He makes ALL things work together for good to those who have been called according to His purpose. (Romans 8:28)

We have to trust that His plans are good, and not evil, even if circumstances seem "bad". Jeremiah 29:11 Or even if people misjudge us and think we are evil.

His time table is not ours! It was seventy years before that particular promise in Jeremiah 29:10 was fulfilled.

When disappointing things happen, seek Him all the more fervently and diligently!

It is His Kingdom, not ours. Trust Him, not outward things.

He is a passionate Person, and He loves us intensely!!

He will reveal the depths of His love to us in ways we have never known, when people condemn us or reject us or despise us.

Those who are wounded get to experience His compassion and delight in them, in ways they never saw before.

He is close to the broken-hearted.

He responds to those who have such a need for healing and realize it. Our grief affects Him so much that He "bottles" our tears and records our lament.

Years ago, someone wrote a song called, "Tears are a Language that God Understands."

Jesus spoke that language when He was here on earth as a human, and was subject to the same temptations and trials that we face.

Have you ever noticed how Jesus would go away by Himself to pray? Hebrews 5:7 tells us that He prayed with tears and strong crying. He was dependent on prayer, even though He was the one who came from Heaven. He received His strength through prayer.

How much more should we. "Trust in him at all times, you people; pour out your hearts to him, for God is our refuge." Psalm 62:8

THE WAY HE SPEAKS

Look at the sky.....God IS speaking.

Volumes.

Psalm 19 tells us that the heavens declare His glory.

The problem is that we have eyes that refuse to see and ears that refuse to hear.

"Do you have eyes but fail to see, and ears but fail to hear?" Mark 8:18

Jesus often said things like, "Whoever has ears to hear, let them hear." Mark 4:9 And "If your eyes are healthy, your whole body will be full of light." Matthew 6:22

We are like deaf people who turn their hearing aids off so they WON'T hear. We turn Him off, and turn to our own ways, because we want our own way.

"Everyone has turned away, all have become corrupt" Psalm 53:3 "We all, like sheep, have gone astray, each of us has turned to our own way" Isaiah 53:6

We are like blind people who follow each other into a ditch. We have no idea how we got there or why. Clueless = blindness. Luke 6:39

Why did Jesus heal blind and deaf people differently? There was one blind man who Jesus healed in stages, and another man had to go and wash his eyes to be healed. Why? Was it some deficiency in Jesus' healing powers? Hardly. Jesus could tell the wind and waves to be still, and they obeyed.

We are not told all the different ways that Jesus healed so many people, only that He did. But the differences in the healings we do know about are puzzling.

I think that it does show us something about Jesus. He thinks of us as individuals, not a lump form of humanity. He could have healed all those people in exactly the same way----He has no limitations.

Yet He chose to show that each person and their situations are unique to Him. He thinks of each person as entirely different from any other. And He delivers us from trouble and rescues us from our dilemmas in as distinctive a fashion as the way He designed us to be one-of-a-kind human beings.

This is something to keep in mind while engaged in ministry---to remind ourselves not to treat people as a lump form of humanity---and to make a way for individual expression and the Lord's unique ways of dealing with people.

The Lord is creative, witty, and imaginative, full of compassion and His goodness is far beyond all comprehension. Ask Him for eyes to see Him as He is....and ears to hear what He is saying.

When He speaks His Word, things happen.....things that are not, suddenly exist. When He speaks His Word and we hear Him, you and I change.....and we see His glory.

"But we all, with unveiled face, beholding as in a mirror the glory of the Lord, are being transformed into the same image from glory to glory, just as from the Lord, the Spirit."
2 Corinthians 3:18 NASB

SECRET INTENTIONS

She came to the dinner party with intentions, and perhaps no one there knew what she planned to do except herself and one other person.

He was aware of her intentions.

She must have kept this a secret from the others, knowing how they might react.

When she broke the alabaster jar, and the scent of perfume pervaded the entire room, everyone knew her secret.

Her action caught them off guard, and there was an immediate stir of unrest and criticism and rebuke. The other disciples were surprised and indignant; they could not sanction such a waste of resources! This perfume was worth a whole year's wages, and she had just poured it all out.

She poured it on Jesus' head, and on His feet.

Jesus reacted in a totally different way, for He knew her secret. In fact, He had planned this long before she ever did it.

"Leave her alone," Jesus replied. "It was intended that she should save this perfume for the day of my burial." John 12:7

He had intentions for Mary. He had given her something precious so that she could pour out her love for Him.

He has intentions for us, as well.

What has He given us that we can pour out to worship Him?

You may not have some perfume that is worth a whole year's wages; you have something more valuable---you have your life. Pour it out at Jesus' feet---and your love for Him will make Him attractive to others.

He knows of our hearts' desire to love Him and to bring Him joy, and He has provided for every one of our needs.

We were created to worship Him and enjoy knowing Him and loving Him; we need this. It is only His love that fulfills us. Mary had discovered this; and she gave Jesus the best that she had. She anointed Him, and because she touched Him, the fragrance clung to her.

When we give Jesus our best, we will be so close to Him that His fragrance will anoint us too. When we pour out our love to Him, He touches us and anoints us.

His love and anointing sustain us.

The alabaster jar had to be broken to release the perfume. There are parts of our lives that must be broken in order for us to worship Him with all our hearts. What is within us is more valuable than what we appear to be.

What is truly important is how Jesus sees us, and not how others see us. We cannot spend our lives trying to live up to the expectations of other people, when Jesus has intentions for us that others may not recognize.

Believe in His intentions, for they are always good.

MORE

Recently Guy and I were watching some documentaries about all the miracles that have happened in Israel since the rebirth of Israel as a nation. That in itself is such a miracle! It is the definite sign that Jesus will be coming soon. Israel is the fig tree in Matthew 24:32-34

Faith sees reality in the things which cannot be seen; but Israel's rebirth is a visible miracle too great to be dismissed by even the most skeptical. So many Old Testament prophecies about Israel have been perfectly fulfilled already! What God says He will do, He does.

"Therefore, since we are receiving a kingdom that cannot be shaken, let us be thankful, and so worship God acceptably with reverence and awe, for our God is a consuming fire." Hebrews 12:28-29

When the kingdom of God becomes more real to us than the world around us---more real than this life---I think we will see even more miracles.

What is worship? Is it just the part of a church service when we sing songs? No, it is the act of expressing our love for Jesus TO HIM, and we should be as fervent and passionate as we possibly can be. How could we be half-hearted in our response to His passion for us?

This is the God who weeps over our tragedy. When Jesus approached Jerusalem, he wept over it. Luke 19:41-44. He knew what was going to happen in 70 A.D. to Jerusalem.

The people there rejected God's gift of salvation through Jesus; they didn't want Him. And so He wept over their loss---and His---for He loved them.

I looked up the Greek word for wept---it was klaio, and it means to weep aloud, expressing uncontainable, audible grief. I see the intensity of his love for people through this.

"Our God is a consuming fire" refers back to Deuteronomy 4:24 which speaks of God as a jealous God who forbids idolatry. I think that some might read this and picture God as someone who has rages of jealousy and burns people up.

I believe that "consuming fire" refers to the passionate love He has for us, and He is the only One who should have that God place in our heart. He will not tolerate "dual occupancy" with some other idolatrous love.

He is an all-or-nothing God when it comes to a relationship with Him. It has to be an intense relationship; His love is our salvation! Correct doctrine alone will not save you. Only an intimacy with Jesus can save us from our selfish way of living and from its consequences.

We pursue that intimacy through His Word and through worship. We see Him in His Word, because He IS the Word. The more we express our adoration to Him in worship, the more real His love will become to us, and the more we will have of Him. He is our heart's desire!

SIDES

The people of Jericho were afraid. They had heard how God opened up the Red Sea for the Israelites to pass through. They heard what God did to two kingdoms east of the Jordan River, and they were terrified.

They stayed in their walled city and hoped that their walls would keep God out.

One woman was more than afraid; she believed. She believed that judgment was coming. She believed that God was coming.

She demonstrated her faith by hiding the two Israelite spies who came into Jericho. She bargained for her life and the lives of her family with these two representatives from God.

They told her to hang a red cord from her window, and her life would be spared, and the lives of the people who were in her house.

When the walls fell, and the Israelite army marched into Jericho, there was the evidence of Rahab's faith: the red cord was hanging from the window.

In our civilization, many do not believe in God's judgment. They think that they can do whatever they want because everything will continue just as it always has. They don't believe that God is coming.

Demons tremble at the thought of God's judgment; they know what is coming. They will not be able to escape that judgment because they are on the side of the devil and they cannot change sides.

The Lord has given us a way of escape; it is through faith.

Rahab took God's side-----she sided with Him, and He took her to His side.

He gave her a heritage with Him. He gave her a Jewish husband who was in the lineage of Christ. Rahab is even named in that lineage in the first chapter of Matthew.

She left her old life behind.

The only way to freedom and safety is in surrender to the Lord through faith in what Jesus has done to rescue us.

WHAT IS TRUE?

There is an expression called "true north". If north is north, what is true north? It's your direction according to the North Pole. And then there's the expression, "true love". How could love not be true, if it's love? What is real truth? How could it be truth if it's not real?

A standard is what you use to measure everything else. God's Word is that standard; the Lord's Word is always what is true. Never be afraid of the Truth---the truth will set you free. (John 8:32)

We have to separate human error from God's nature, by reflecting on the character of God as it is portrayed in the Scriptures. It may take a while to realize that the Lord is not thinking of us the way that people have.

Human opinion is not synonymous with God's truth. We need to agree with God, not the other way around. The essence of humility is agreeing with God, and not insisting that He agree with us. He is always right in His verdict.

"Against you, you only, have I sinned and done what is evil in your sight; so you are right in your verdict and justified when you judge." Psalm 51:4

The wisdom and insight from God's Word will help us understand what is right and just and fair. Proverbs 2:1-9 His truth will protect us. Proverbs 2:11

Help us Lord never to discount what You are doing, in favor of our own preferences.

Now, we see only a dim reflection of reality; our knowledge is limited and imperfect. In eternity, we will be able to see things and know perfectly----even as we are known and seen by the Lord now. We are fully and clearly known and understood by God now.

"For now we see only a reflection as in a mirror; then we shall see face to face. Now I know in part; then I shall know fully, even as I am fully known." 1 Corinthians 13:12

Not until eternity will we see and know like that. So we must trust His love for people, not our own assessments. "Therefore judge nothing before the appointed time." 1 Corinthians 4:5 The Lord isn't finished with us or with others, so don't judge His work. We can trust that He will complete what He started in us.

"being confident of this, that he who began a good work in you will carry it on to completion until the day of Christ Jesus." Philippians 1:6

This is the example Jesus gave us: He did not live to please himself; His judgements were only what came from the Father. "By myself I can do nothing; I judge only as I hear, and my judgment is just, for I seek not to please myself but him who sent me." John 5:30

He knows the end from the beginning!!!! Isaiah 46:10

All truth is in Jesus: He IS the truth.

Jesus is the way, the truth, and the life. John 14:6

THE GIFTS OF CHRISTMAS:
THE REMEDY

The very first two humans ever created made a choice of such cataclysmic effects, that there is only one remedy which could ever reverse those consequences.

This decision once acted upon, caused world-wide devastation, upheavals in nature, and changed the very character of mankind from its original design.

Suffering and pain were unheard of until that day.

The remedies that people think of are no solution for the problem of sin and its effects.

Trying to "be good" does not and cannot eliminate or reverse the results of that choice.

Trying to be good enough or do enough "good deeds" to merit salvation is like putting a Band-Aid on a person experiencing heart failure.

It is no help for our dilemma---no cure for the disease which is destroying us.

How absurd to think that the corrupted nature of mankind could ever produce a remedy!

Then.... there was Christmas.

In the Father's plan, this Baby could not have the inherited genetic DNA mutated by sin, so the Son of God was not formed in Mary's womb through human conception.

Jesus' life and His death on the Cross, are the only remedy which can reverse the consequences of sin in our lives.

….if we believe.

The deceiver robbed us the first time in the Garden of Eden; don't let it happen to you again!

Don't let the enemy trick you out of the truth.

Though you have heard the Christmas story so many times, don't let the enemy disillusion you to the remedy God has given.

Jesus came to save us.

"how shall we escape if we ignore so great a salvation? This salvation, which was first announced by the Lord, was confirmed to us by those who heard him. God also testified to it by signs, wonders and various miracles, and by gifts of the Holy Spirit distributed according to his will." Hebrews 2:3-4

Believe in Him.

He is our only remedy.

THE GIFTS OF CHRISTMAS: VICTORY

Hindsight is foresight. That is, we can learn from the past. Mistakes and errors are recorded in the Bible for that reason.

We can study our opponent and we should. He has surely studied our weaknesses. If you have not yet realized that you have such a dedicated adversary, wake up! I Peter 5:8

In the Garden of Eden, the enemy insinuated that God is not trustworthy---that He is devious. This enemy projects his own evil character traits onto God; he blames God for the things of which he is guilty.

People who are caught in his traps often emulate this; they do the same thing. They accuse you of the same wrong that they are doing, to hide and evade their own guilt.

It has taken me a long time to recognize that it is not the Holy Spirit who uses shame to torment us. I used to confuse this with the conviction of the Holy Spirit. The enemy tricks us, and when we fall, he uses shame to keep us from God's presence.

When the Holy Spirit convicts, it is different. He is straightforward, gentle, never abusive, and always directs us to reconciliation. Derisive, demeaning, derogatory---this is not the attitude of the Holy Spirit or how He speaks.

God is in the business of restoration, not condemnation. He did not rant or yell or speak abusively to Adam and Eve; He made clothes for them, and gave them a promise of deliverance. He would one day sacrifice Himself for their offspring.

How great is our God! How merciful and compassionate He is! He does not treat us as our sins deserve. (Psalm 103:10)

He is kind, and wants to help us overcome. The enemy makes us feel that God despises us. Nothing could be further from the truth. (Romans 8:32)

However, to those who defy Him, and resist the Holy Spirit, the Lord is fearsome and dreadful. He is the Lion of Judah! He cannot be manipulated or coerced in any way; He is absolutely sovereign. Do not attempt to play games with a lion!

God's Word is pure, and it will purify us if we allow it. Often, preconceived notions come from human nature and camouflage the true meaning of the Scriptures.

Our past alters our perceptions. "I pray that the eyes of your heart may be enlightened in order that you may know the hope to which he has called you…" Ephesians 1:18

He is calling out to us, just as He did in the Garden of Eden. The enemy intends for you to fail; the Lord intends for you to have victory. Whose voice will you listen to and follow?

"…This is the victory that has overcome the world, even our faith." I John 5:4

That first Christmas was the beginning of victory.

THE GIFTS OF CHRISTMAS: FELLOWSHIP RESTORED

In the beginning of creation, the Lord walked with Adam and Eve in the garden, and they enjoyed fellowship. This was lost, when Adam and Eve traded God's truth for Satan's lies.

Then that long awaited Christmas came, and our days of separation were over.

God did not send His Son into the world just to pay the penalty for our sin, and then leave us to ourselves.

God did not send His Son into the world to give us a doctrine or a set of rules.

He shared His Son with us so that we could have an intimate relationship with the most wonderful Person in the universe!

His Son identified with us by not only taking on human form, but by becoming human. He experienced our needs----except that He did not have the sin factor. He was the second Adam; the perfect Adam----one who never knew sin.

"But you know that he appeared so that he might take away our sins. And in him is no sin." 1 John 3:5

"For the joy set before him he endured the cross, scorning its shame, and sat down at the right hand of the throne of God." Hebrews 12:2

What was this joy that motivated Him to endure such pain and cruelty, ignominy and abasement? It was His love for us, and His desire to be with us.

Satan does his utmost to obscure this love and prevent us from knowing it. But once we have found this Love, nothing outside of us can ever separate us again from the love of God that is in Christ Jesus!

"For I am convinced that neither death nor life, neither angels nor demons, neither the present nor the future, nor any powers, neither height nor depth, nor anything else in all creation, will be able to separate us from the love of God that is in Christ Jesus our Lord." Romans 8:38-39

The gift from the Father was not just the sacrificial death of His Son; it was the gift of a relationship.

Jesus Himself is our Gift.

God gave us His Son.

THE GIFTS OF CHRISTMAS: NO FEAR

The first message of Christmas was, "Do not be afraid."

When the angel came to Mary to tell her of God's plan, he said: "Do not be afraid." Luke 1:30

Even before that, an angel came to the priest who would become the father of John the Baptist. The angel said, "Do not be afraid, Zechariah…" Luke 1:13

On the night Jesus was born, the angel told the shepherds "Do not be afraid…." Luke 2:10

When Joseph, who was engaged to Mary, was troubled over this unexpected pregnancy, an angel spoke to him in a dream and said, "Joseph son of David, do not be afraid…." Matthew 1:20

In all of these situations, the Lord reassured them that He was in charge of their lives; He had a plan they could trust. He was carrying out His plan, so there was no need to be afraid.

Now when we hear those words repeated in the Christmas story, has it become only a salutation….or rhetoric? Does it seem to be "story language"--- like, "Once upon a time…"?

The Lord does not use empty words. He means what He says, and He says what He means.

Though I have been walking with the Lord for over forty years now, I have been afraid at times. During these times, I sensed an underlying uneasiness that somehow, some unrealized sin that I was unaware of, would give me a nasty surprise in the end, and that I would be turned away at Heaven's Gate.

At these times, I felt obligated to continue holding onto this anxious wariness, fearful that I would neglect or overlook the conviction of the Holy Spirit without it.

What I did not realize is that this attitude is based on fear and not on trust in the Lord's character. "God is light; in him there is no darkness at all." 1 John 1:5

He does not change like shifting shadows. (James 1:17)

"But if we walk in the light, as he is in the light, we have fellowship with one another, and the blood of Jesus, his Son, purifies us from all sin." 1 John 1:7

The enemy would like us to think of the Lord as a capricious person---as someone who would disqualify you if you unknowingly offended him. This keeps our hearts in fear and bondage.

If we understand God's character, then our hearts are secure. We can say with confidence:

"The Lord is my shepherd, I shall not want......I will fear no evil; for You are with me; Your rod and Your staff, they comfort me." Psalm 23:1, 4 NKJV

The Lord is looking after us! He has given us everything that we need for life and godliness. (2 Peter 1:3)

He is not waiting for us to fall into sin so he can condemn us; He wants us to depend on His love, His light, and His goodness to keep us free from sin!

A habit of dependence on Him depends on a habit of prayer and reading His Word. This habit gives us confidence in our relationship with Him.

"There is no fear in love. But perfect love drives out fear, because fear has to do with punishment. The one who fears is not made perfect in love." 1 John 4:18

That first Christmas brought His light to our darkness, and His perfect love to our fearful hearts.

THE GIFTS OF CHRISTMAS: THE HOLY SPIRIT

Adam and Eve lived in a pure and perfect world, untouched by the effects of sin. And yet they were deceived by the enemy, and lost everything.

We live in a world tainted and corrupted by sin; we are much more vulnerable to deception.

This is why it was vital that the Lord sent the Holy Spirit after He returned to Heaven. He promised that He would not leave us like defenseless orphans. John 14:16-18

The Holy Spirit was the agent at Creation. In Genesis 1:2, we see the Holy Spirit "hovering over the waters". He was waiting. Then the commands of God came forth, and Creation began. God's Word---His commands---took shape and form and became reality on the earth.

When the God of the universe became a human baby, it was the Holy Spirit's doings. The Word became flesh in Mary through the power of the Holy Spirit. John 1:1 and John 1:14

We are regenerated—reborn---by the power of the Holy Spirit when we believe in Jesus. John 1:12-13

It is the Holy Spirit who makes God's Word become a reality to us, as well.

We need to "take in" more of God's Word continually. What you ingest spiritually becomes who you are. Lord, let Your Word become who we are.....birth Your truth in us.

The Holy Spirit is our helper in all of this. The "natural" man does not grasp the truths of God's Kingdom because they are spiritually understood. We must have the Holy Spirit inside of us, and become supernatural people, led by the Spirit. I Corinthians 2:14

It is the Holy Spirit who reveals and identifies Jesus as the Son of God. He revealed Him to an old man named Simeon, who had been waiting for the Messiah's birth. Luke 2:26

It was the Holy Spirit who identified the Son of God to John the Baptist. John 1:32-34

And the Spirit reveals Him to us. John 16:13-15

Our relationship with God begins and finishes with God's Word---Jesus is the Alpha and Omega---the beginning and the completion of all things. Revelation 1:8

"Be filled with the Spirit....." Ephesians 5:18

And Christmas will be Christmas to you!

THE GIFTS OF CHRISTMAS: HIS KINGDOM

Children are still enthralled by stories of princes and princesses, castles and kingdoms.

I think we all are. There is something in us that longs for this.

God has given us a Kingdom; not of this world, but from His. John 18:36 It is a holy Kingdom, full of light and power. Colossians 1:12 The language of this Kingdom is Love.

It is invisible to the "natural" eye at this time, but we can see its effects. We can know its King---He becomes the Ruler of our hearts when we surrender to Him. Colossians 1:13

He shares His wealth and splendor with us; he confers on us His Kingdom. Luke 22:29 He gives us this inheritance in an ever-Living, everlasting Will! I Peter 1:3-5

We demonstrate our citizenship in this Kingdom through giving of the tithe. This is the portion of our income that belongs to the Kingdom.

Our King does not need earthly goods; but we need to pledge our allegiance to Him through the tithe. It is the holy dedicated offering from our lifework.

It would be a sacrilege to spend it on ourselves, and the King cannot bless disobedience. He has promised that blessings and His favor will be ours when we obey the principles of His Kingdom. Matthew 6:33, Malachi 3:10

Tithing protects our hearts from the danger of allowing money to rule us instead of the King. Tithing shows that we respect and reverence and trust our King above all others.

This act of faith in Him promotes His Kingdom---where we live---in the natural realm. It is an act of worship---a giving of ourselves, and the fruit of our labor. Hebrews 12:28

In Genesis 4, we see that Cain did not follow the Lord's instructions concerning giving of himself---he followed his own desires. He subsequently lost the divine protection for his heart and became full of jealousy, anger, and rage. Instead of an act of worship, he committed an act of murder---and was banished.

Many years later, the King Himself came down into this pit of angry, murderous humanity---He was born in an obscure village in a dark unknown corner of the world.

A Light shone out from there---a Light from Heaven---and the darkness in this world has never been able to put it out. John 1:4-5 And it never shall.

This is the Light of the Kingdom of God. And He invites you into His Kingdom! Luke 12:32

Come into His Kingdom this Christmas, and know Him....

His light is for us.

THE GIFTS OF CHRISTMAS:
A NEW SONG

Have you ever admired a very musical family, and wished you were born into that family?

When you surrender your life to Christ---and He adopts you as His child---you become a part of a very musical family! The Scriptures tell us that He rejoices over you with singing! Zephaniah 3:17

At the dawn of creation, even the stars sang! Job 38:7 Scientists now confirm that the universe is not silent---the planets are "humming," so to speak.

Christmas brings us a new song!

After the angel gave his message to Mary, she went to see her cousin Elizabeth, who was now pregnant, though her womb had been dead through age. The Holy Spirit came on Elizabeth and she recognized that Mary was with child---the Messiah!

And Mary sang a new song-----of praise to the Lord.

Elizabeth's husband had been unable to speak due to his doubt of the angel's message to him. When Elizabeth gave birth to a son, Zechariah communicated that the baby's name was John---and suddenly Zechariah could speak. In that instant, God gave him a new song!

When the angels appeared to the shepherds, one angel delivered a message from Heaven. Some say the angels didn't sing---but the Scriptures tell us that a host of angels praised God. Since praise is often musical, I can't help but imagine that the angels sang.

Christmas is a new song!

"The Lord is my Strength and Song; and He has become my Salvation." Psalm 118:14 AMPC

"He put a new song in my mouth, a hymn of praise to our God. Many will see and fear the Lord and put their trust in him." Psalm 40:3

Have you lost your life-song?-----or have you never found it?

Find it in Christ this Christmas!

"Sing and make music from your heart to the Lord" Ephesians 5:19

THE GIFTS OF CHRISTMAS:
A STAR TO FOLLOW

We went to see one of the new Star Wars movies together; it was a family event.

The very first Star Wars film came out the year Guy and I were married, so we're a bit sentimental about the original group of characters.

I really enjoyed observing the directing skill in this new film; I noticed the interesting viewpoints he gives to the audience through the camera angles---this pulls you into the story. I appreciate how he captured the "nostalgic feel" of an older Star Wars film.

In this movie, everyone is looking for something: for a family and a father-figure; a lost son; freedom from a tyrannical government; a hidden mentor; help in the battle against evil, and as always, someone is seeking self-exalting power.

And while they are searching, one character discovers the mysterious power called the "force".

I am so thankful that the Lord is not an inanimate "force" that can be manipulated and used, or that has to be appeased and balanced, as in "yin yang". He is a Person that we can actually know.

Better than that, He is the Hero that we have always longed for. We don't need to follow a movie star or a well-known celebrity….those wise men gave us the best example. Jesus is the Star to follow…..He is the most magnificent Person in this vast universe....and wonder of all wonders, He is now looking for us!

That is what Christmas is all about.

You may feel like a disconnected person stranded in some dismal deserted place on this dusty planet, sifting through junk just trying to make a living. Jesus is trying to get your attention; He is communicating with you, if you will just notice His signals.

He speaks to us through the legacy of His Word.

We are the abandoned orphans, the unwanted ones, the ones left while others are chosen for great acclaim or glamour in the world. Jesus wants US; He wants to adopt us and make us His heirs. This is the greatest rags-to-riches story in the history of mankind.

Ephesians 1:5, Romans 8:15

And we will know His victory; in fact, we can be part of it! He makes us into warriors for His truth. (Psalm 18:34)

There is coming a time of great triumph and celebration, and we are invited to celebrate with Him, in His victory! This great gathering will be a commemoration of our relationship with Him. (Matthew 8:11, Revelation 19:9)

I hope you will pick up His invitation, read it, and accept it....it is in His Word.

"Yet to all who did receive him, to those who believed in his name, he gave the right to become children of God--" John 1:12

THE GIFTS OF CHRISTMAS:
THE ANOINTING

When the Lord gives an assignment, He also gives an anointing to equip us for the task.

The earliest record of this in the Bible is in Exodus 35:30-35, when the Lord gave Bezalel and Oholiab the skills needed to design and make the Tabernacle and its furnishings.

I think it is within reason to believe that Abraham operated under this anointing when he armed his household servants, and they went out to battle an army of skilled warriors. (Genesis 14)

They fought this marauding army, defeated them, and rescued all those who had been taken as captives. It was after this event that the priest Melchizedek came to Abraham and blessed him. (Melchizedek resembles Jesus)

I believe that Mary and Joseph were given an anointing by the Holy Spirit to go through the shame and repulsion they must have endured by those who did not believe their story; that Elizabeth and Zechariah were given an anointing to raise John the Baptist to be the forerunner for the Messiah; and that Anna and Simeon were given an anointing to tell others in the Temple, about Jesus.

And I believe the shepherds were given an anointing to tell all that they met, about the Savior they found in the manger....and the wise men were given an anointing to find the Christ child.

All of these people participated in the Lord's story, and He is calling you and me to participate in His story today.

There is a big difference between having pride in one's own accomplishments, and having confidence in what the Lord has enabled you to do. There is a big difference between exalting your talents, and rejoicing in the gifts God has given you to use for His glory.

The difference is the anointing of the Holy Spirit.

The anointing of God gives our lives significance. Living for self is a dead end; but when we are working with the Lord, for His purposes in the earth, the anointing makes God's presence real to other people and to us as well.

Don't hide from Him; hide IN Him. He will "take you under His wing" and cover you with His feathers. His love covers our offenses. Psalm 91:4, 1 Peter 4:8 His love shields us from harboring an offended spirit.

The Holy Spirit is at the same time, our Comforter and our trainer. He trains us to battle against the forces of darkness. He refreshes us and restores our soul when we are battle-weary. Psalm 23:2-3

We must depend on the Holy Spirit and not our own personal preferences. He is the Leader in this holy army of servants. We will rescue many captives---including some who are from our own families. And when it is all over, Jesus will meet us and bless us.

And our hearts will be merry, in His joy.

Merry Christmas!!!

THE GIFTS OF CHRISTMAS---ESTEEM

The Lord is searching the earth for those who have faith, and when He finds it, He treasures it. Faith and trust in Him is extremely valuable to the Lord. Luke 18:8

Yet we can't produce it ourselves; faith comes through the message of God's Word. Faith comes when we "take Him at His Word"----it comes from believing that He, more than any other, is a Person who keeps His word.

"Even if everyone else is a liar, God is true." Romans 3:4 NLT

"Consequently, faith comes from hearing the message, and the message is heard through the word about Christ." Romans 10:17

Faith gives us confidence that He is FOR us---He is not against us. We begin to see how He values us.

"Are not two sparrows sold for a penny? Yet not one of them will fall to the ground outside your Father's care. And even the very hairs of your head are all numbered. So don't be afraid; you are worth more than many sparrows."

Matthew 10:29-31

Your life has purpose in the Kingdom of God; your participation is needed and desired. This is the gift of esteem; you are valued by God.

Your contribution is valuable. The Lord does not enlist us to be on His team only to sit on the bench. He intends us to play in the game.

The Holy Spirit is our trainer; submit to the discipline of Bible study and prayer, and exercise your faith by giving of yourself, your abilities, and your resources.

This life has meaning when you use it to invest in eternity. Jesus is our Eternity; knowing Him is eternal life. John 17:3

He gives our lives significance through our participation with Him in His plans. This is how prayer is a gift and privilege; we participate in His plans through prayer.

The God who created the universe did not need David's slingshot to take down a giant; but David did. The Lord gave David's life significance through the faith he exercised.

When we do things to promote God's Kingdom, His goodness makes us look good as well!

Everything about the Lord is GOOD.

He has no dark side at all.

"This is the message we have heard from him and declare to you: God is light; in him there is no darkness at all." 1 John 1:5

"Every good and perfect gift is from above, coming down from the Father of the heavenly lights, who does not change like shifting shadows." James 1:17

THE GIFTS OF CHRISTMAS:
THE FOUNDATION

We find the foundation for our lives in Christmas....

...Not in the lights or festivities, nor in the family gatherings and memories---not even in the acts of goodwill exhibited towards people....

We find it in the fact that God sent His Son into the world to rescue us.

The culture of the world has nothing to build on; all that it has is competition and jealousy, selfish desires and strife, lust and greed. These ambitions are not stable or permanent.

"The world and its desires pass away, but whoever does the will of God lives forever." 1 John 2:17

In Christ, we are being made into a habitation---a sanctuary--for God's presence; it is built on the Word of God and the people who believed Him. He wants to dwell with us again, as He did in the Garden.

"Consequently, you are no longer foreigners and strangers, but fellow citizens with God's people and also members of his household, built on the foundation of the apostles and prophets, with Christ Jesus himself as the chief cornerstone. In him the whole building is joined together and rises to become a holy temple in the Lord." Ephesians 2:19-21

We are no longer outcasts from His presence, sent away from the Garden.

"And in him you too are being built together to become a dwelling in which God lives by his Spirit." Ephesians 2:22

Our home is in Jesus; we belong to Him.

 "you also, like living stones, are being built into a spiritual house to be a holy priesthood, offering spiritual sacrifices acceptable to God through Jesus Christ." 1 Peter 2:5

People who belong to the world's culture try to build their lives on goals and striving; they are striving for the top position, or striving to be thought better than anyone else, or striving to be "somebody", or striving to prove themselves right and others wrong.

There is only One who is right. All the rest of us will always get it wrong without His rightness. There is only one foundation that is right for us.

"For no one can lay any foundation other than the one already laid, which is Jesus Christ." 1 Corinthians 3:11

We live with so much competition in this world that it is almost impossible to imagine a world completely void of it! Heaven will be that place.

The only one there who had lustful ambition for dominance and power was thrown out of heaven; that is how Lucifer became Satan. This is the cause of turmoil on our planet, for when he left heaven, he came here.

So we must choose our building materials carefully, as we build upon the foundation of Christ. The enemy will suggest we use what the world favors, but this is only wood, hay and straw. Ask the Lord to give you His "gold, silver, and precious jewels" to build with….these can be found in His Word….these are the things that will last.

"If anyone builds on this foundation using gold, silver, costly stones, wood, hay or straw, their work will be shown for what it is, because the Day will bring it to light. It will be revealed with fire, and the fire will test the quality of each person's work." 1 Corinthians 3:12-13

Jesus is the Master builder; under His supervision, the work will be Quality.

THE GIFTS OF CHRISTMAS: PREPARATION FOR CELEBRATION

It's that time again; time to take down the Christmas decorations. Does it make you feel kind of sad---as if you are packing up the joy, hope, and excitement that Christmas brings?

It's exciting to prepare for Christmas; I can't imagine a world without Christmas....that would be a world without hope. I think that is why it is disappointing to take everything down and put it away. These things represent such a time of hope.

But we are not packing up our hope. God Himself is preparing for a tremendous celebration---it will be the culmination of all the hopes of every Christmas.

And the invitation is in His Word; everyone who is willing is invited to come! This is the great banquet that Jesus talked about in Matthew 8, Luke 13, and Revelation 19:9. We will be celebrating all that Jesus has done to rescue the people He loves---and that includes us!

We will be celebrating the One who is our Hope---our Joy---our Future. He loves us, and has chosen us to belong to Him. He is still inviting....accept Him now as your Savior....before it is too late.

Nothing compares to what we have to look forward to when we belong to Jesus. Nothing, absolutely nothing, compares to what God is preparing for those who love Him. 1 Cor. 2:9

His story is not over; come be part of it!
The best part is yet to come.

ABOUT THE AUTHOR

Teresa Lavergne resides in Louisiana with her husband Guy. They were involved with children's ministry for many years and have written many materials for ministry. Some of these have been published under the title of Act Upon a Story and are currently sold through Amazon. Teresa has also written a children's fiction book, which is an allegory entitled The Angel in the Garden, also marketed through Amazon.

www.ingramcontent.com/pod-product-compliance
Lightning Source LLC
Chambersburg PA
CBHW071212090426
42736CB00014B/2791